CHURCH WALKS

IN THE

YORKSHIRE DALES

Published by Sigma Leisure - an imprint of Sigma Press, Stobart House, Pontyclerc, Penybanc Road, Ammanford, Carmarthenshire SA18 3HP.

British Library Cataloguing in Publication Data
A CIP record for this book is available from the British Library.

ISBN:978-1-91075-825-0

Typesetting and Design by: Sigma Press, Ammanford.

Cover photograph: St. Owswalds, Horton-in-Ribblesdale

Photographs: © Peter Naldrett unless stated otherwise.

Maps: Sigma Press
Contains OS data © Crown copyright [and database right] 2016

Printed by: Akcent Media Ltd.

CHURCH WALKS
IN THE
YORKSHIRE DALES

PETER NALDRETT & REV. KATE BOTTLEY

SIGMA Leisure

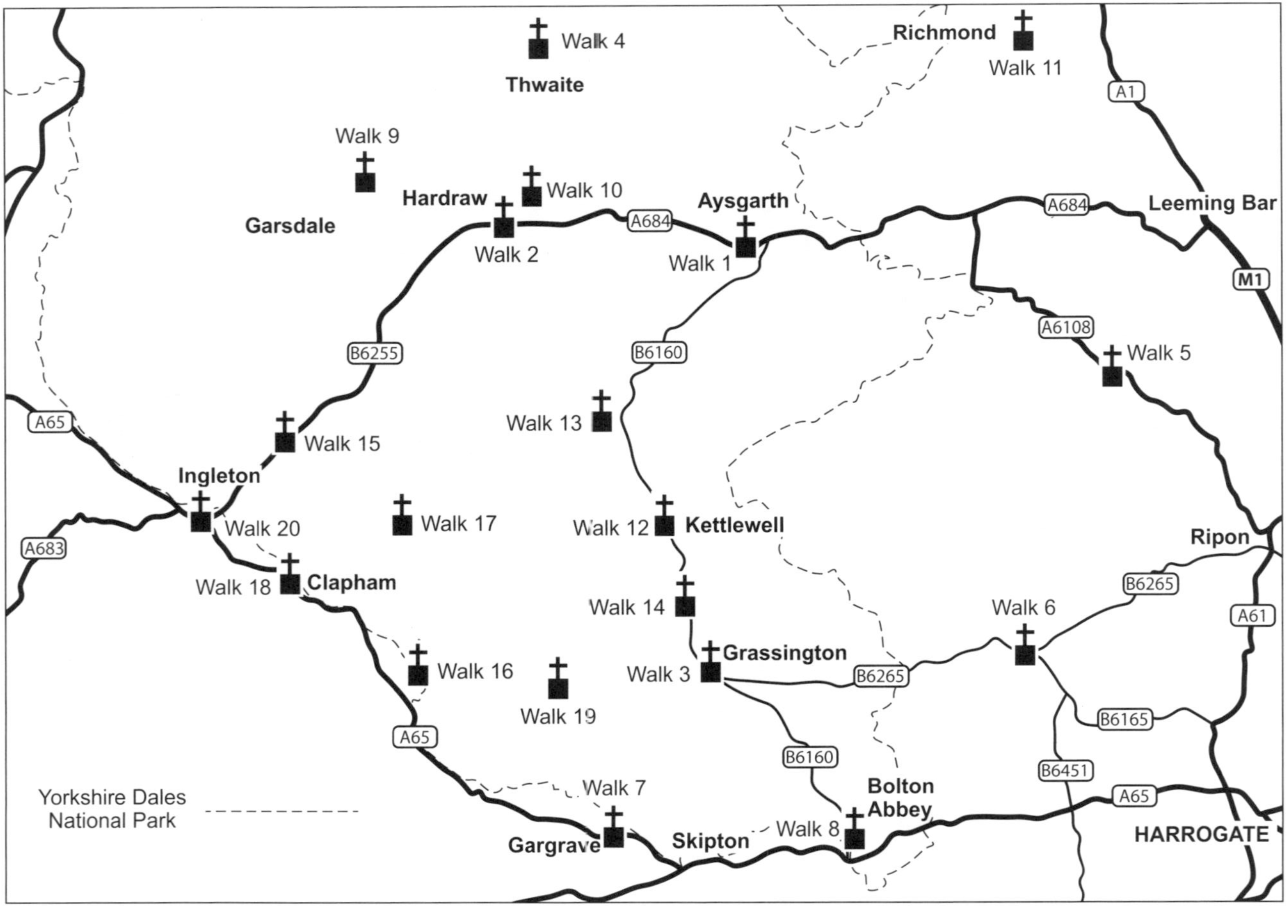
Walk 4
Thwaite
Richmond
Walk 11
A1
Walk 9
Walk 10
Hardraw
Garsdale
A684
Aysgarth
Walk 2
Walk 1
A684
Leeming Bar
M1
A6108
Walk 5
B6255
B6160
Walk 13
A65
Walk 15
Ingleton
Walk 20
Walk 17
Walk 12
Kettlewell
Ripon
A683
Walk 18
Clapham
B6265
Walk 14
Walk 6
A61
Grassington
Walk 3
Walk 16
Walk 19
B6265
B6165
A65
B6160
B6451
Walk 7
Bolton Abbey
A65
Yorkshire Dales National Park
Walk 8
HARROGATE
Gargrave
Skipton

CONTENTS

For Nicola, Toby, Willow and Neil. Thanks for joining me on the walks.

Peter Naldrett

For Graham, who likes walking and churches more than I do, and Ruby and Arthur, who don't.

Rev. Kate Bottley

INTRODUCTION

Along with the Rev. Kate Bottley, it's been an absolute pleasure researching, walking and writing in preparation for this book. The Yorkshire Dales is a phenomenally beautiful part of the country with no shortage of cracking walks to embark on. Waterfalls, hills and valleys; the Dales has the finest in the land. There are also dozens of brilliant towns and villages to explore, each with its own charm and character. And, of course, at the heart of many of these is a church, still the centre of community life in so many places. What we've tried to do in this book is introduce you to the Yorkshire Dales through these places of worship, using them as a starting point to explore the traditions and physical beauty of the Dales. You'll be able to go inside and investigate many of the churches, learn about their history, trek through the wonderful surrounding countryside and then stop for a cuppa (or something a bit stronger) in one of the many excellent cafes and pubs. We think it's a great way to get to know the Dales and we hope you have much fun exploring the churches and hills of North Yorkshire.

Of course, it's important that you prepare fully for all the walks in this book. That means wearing a sturdy pair of walking boots, taking drinks and snacks and making sure you're dressed for the weather. This means you'll have to check the weather before you set out and ensure you're thoroughly prepared for what's to come, especially if the forecast isn't good. The weather can turn in the Yorkshire Dales really quickly and you should be cautious and well prepared. Take a phone and make sure it's fully charged, along with a GPS device if you have one. Most importantly, though, take a map. The maps in this book are meant only as a guide to help you on your way and you should take the relevant Ordnance Survey map with you to monitor your route and make sure you know the way ahead.

The time I've spent in the Yorkshire Dales researching and writing this collection of lovely walks has been delightful. There are so many wonderful views, but also a great deal of heritage to discover and celebrate. What makes this walking book stand out from others, though, is the contribution from Rev. Bottley. You might know her from TV appearances on the likes of

Gogglebox and *Songs of Praise*, or from her thoughtful musings on BBC Radio 2. Although much of Rev. Kate's work sees her speaking to millions of people, the core of her work as a vicar is based around speaking to individuals at a key point in their lives. Here, her Thought for the Walks are aimed directly at you – on the specific walk you are setting out on. She raises key questions for you to think about and discuss. And I hope you'll agree that they give these Yorkshire Dales church-based strolls an extra dimension.

Enjoy your time in the Dales, and may you return here again and again.

Peter Naldrett

WALK 1
Aysgarth

A stunning church with a waterfalls walk to match it, Aysgarth is a gem of the northern Dales.

What you need to know	
Distance	4km/2.4 miles
Time taken	1 hour 30 minutes
Starting point	From the A684, follow the signs for Aysgarth Falls. Park at the National Park Visitor centre. Grid reference SE 011, 887
Difficulty	A steep climb at the end, but otherwise a well signed and simple route
Refreshments	Along the walk you'll pass the Mill Race Tea Shop, a nice spot for a drink and bite to eat. Tel: 01969 663446 www.themillraceteashop.co.uk Postcode: DL8 3SR
Map	OS Explorer OL30: Yorkshire Dales North and Central Area

St Andrew's Church, Aysgarth

When you go up to look at the church, you'll no doubt be struck by how big the churchyard is. Welcome to the largest churchyard in the country, home to a church that dates back over 1,000 years and has seen a wealth of historic events over the centuries. Now a Grade II listed building, you won't be surprised to learn that this tall and mighty building is not the same one that has graced the site for the last millennium. We know that the original church was rebuilt in 1536 and that a significant restoration project took place in 1866.

Within the building there is more history to explore, not least in the screen that was originally found in Jervaulx Abbey but was taken away to the church in the 1530s as the Dissolution of the Monasteries was ordered by King Henry

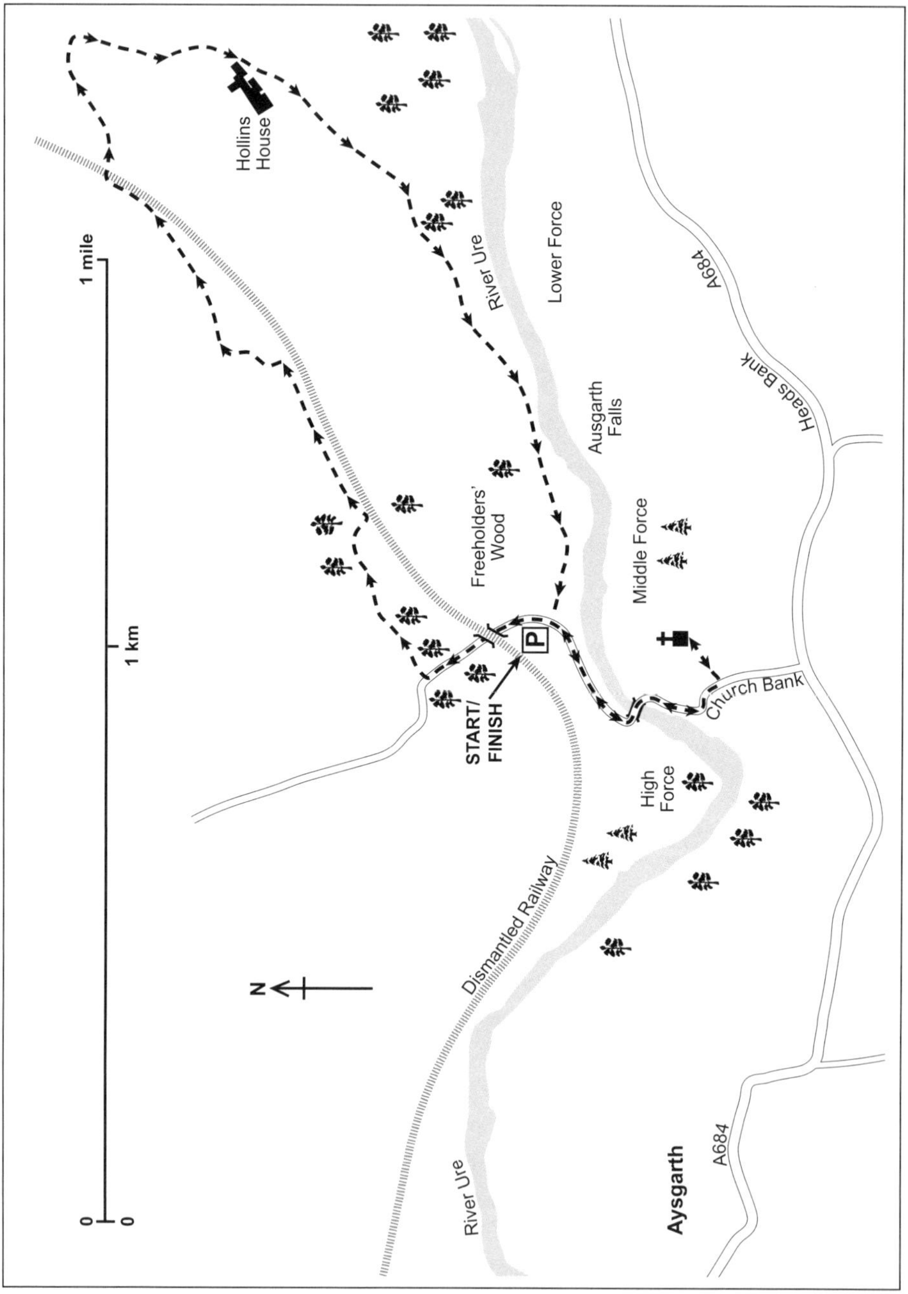
1 mile
1 km
0
0
N
Hollins House
River Ure
Lower Force
A684
Heads Bank
Ausgarth Falls
Freeholders' Wood
Middle Force
START/ FINISH
P
Church Bank
High Force
Dismantled Railway
River Ure
Aysgarth
A684

VIII. It's a great place to explore alongside your walk that investigates the three stages of Aysgarth Falls.

The church has fabulous, therapeutic company in the valley, both visually with the dramatic falls and also mentally as the distant roar of the water rings out like the crashing background side-effects of a self-help relaxation CD. At one time, there would have been a harmonious whistling of steam engines added to the soundtrack as they rattled by here en route to Hawes. But don't presume that the railway has given way for ever; there are groups interested in getting it open again and using new tracks to transport thousands of tourists into Aysgarth.

Route

The easiest place to park to explore the amazing parish church of St Andrews and the brilliant waterfalls nearby is the National Park Visitor Centre. The pay and display car park has plenty of room and gets you away from the bustle of the main road.

The visitor centre

From here (grid reference SE 011, 887), walk away from the visitor centre towards the back of the car park and follow the signs for the upper falls. This will bring you out at a local road and you should cross the bridge, looking out for the upper falls away to your right. Once you cross the bridge you'll pass the Mill Race Café on the left, which is a good place for some refreshments, but the walk continues on the path at the side of the road, climbing all the way up the hill until you reach the entrance to the church on the left.

Explore the churchyard and the breath-taking surroundings, all the while listening out for the roar of the waterfalls you can hear in the distance. Return to the road and make your way down the hill, crossing the bridge and retracing your steps up the visitor centre.

The church in the background at Aysgarth Falls

Our walk is not complete now, however. Make your way to the opposite side of the car park and cross over the road, picking up the path at the other side. Once you're through the gate, the path forks in two and you should take the path off to the left, passing through Freeholders' Wood. A gate takes you into the next wooded areas, though the trees aren't as thick here and it eventually brings you up to the old railway bridge.

Go through the bridge and through the gates on the other side, turning right and continuing along a track. Take the path that is signed off the track to the right and cross over the field. Cross another wooded area and turn right when it brings you out onto a track (grid reference SE 020, 895).

You'll see the track is blocked off and you are sent along the path to the left, which you should follow to the end of the field. But before you reach the far wall, take the path that sort of doubles back to the right. This takes you through Hollins House, and you should follow this route as it takes you across fields and through gates, eventually turning left and going down to the River Ure on the left.

This final stretch of the walk is superb; make sure you follow the path but take in the signposted diversions off to the left to take in the middle falls and lower falls. Across the river from this point you'll be able to get a great view of the church, with the fantastic building lying in the background and the noisy, crashing falls in the foreground. When you're finished, head along the path and you'll end up at the road, with the visitor centre lying across the road to the right. Make you way back to the car park, where you set out from.

Rev. Kate Bottley's Thought For The Walk

Mine's a pint!

You can tell a lot by a place from its pubs. My own village where I live, despite only having a population of about 900, has four pubs. Until recently, it was six. No, we are not a village of hopeless old soaks, but rather one on an ancient coaching route. The community of Asygarth is the same, situated on the direct route of the coaches that passed through on their way north and south. In the 17th century the village pub 'The George and Dragon' began its life offering to weary travellers a place to rest for the night and to get something to eat. Perhaps also something to drink before starting out on the road again in the morning. Today 'The George' is a grade II listed building serving the local ale from the Black Sheep brewery.

In more recent years the village offered hospitality of a different sort to the riders and teams of the Tour de France which passed through the village on 5th July 2014. Ask around and the folk in the village will tell you first hand of what that experience was like. The same spirit of encouragement for the journey ahead and refreshment after the journey was very much in evidence.

The village offers a place of spiritual hospitality, too, with its church, two chapels and Quaker meeting house, although not all of these are open for worship anymore.

Offering hospitality to weary travellers is a strong tradition not only in the Christian faith but in all religions and beliefs. The practice not only blesses the one receiving hospitality but also the one providing it. Allowing others to host you when you are weary from the journey is a spiritual discipline.

Questions to think about along the way

When have you received hospitality?
When have you offered hospitality?
What was the best place you have ever stayed? What was the worst?
Have you ever been on a pilgrimage?

WALK 2
Hawes

In the heart of Wensleydale, sample the rolling hills and the odd bit of cheese as well!

What you need to know	
Distance	7 km/4.3 miles
Time taken	2 hours
Starting point	You'll find a car park off the main street in the centre of Hawes. Then make your way down to St Margaret's Church, opposite the White Hart Inn. Grid reference: SD 873, 898
Difficulty	Take care in wet weather, but these local paths are generally straight forward
Refreshments	The walk goes by the Wensleydale Creamery, a place you simply have to pop into. Aside from cheese samples, there's a nice little museum and a café to have a rest. Tel: 01969 667664 www.wensleydale.co.uk Postcode: DL8 3RN
Map	OS Explorer OL30: Yorkshire Dales North and Central Area

Hawes

Set back from the main road and dominating the skyline in this picturesque rural village, St Margaret's Church is a thriving place of worship as well as being an attractive tourist attraction. Going back a couple of centuries, the church on this site was much smaller and known as a 'chapel of ease'. These were essentially rural chapels built to help those who were too far away from the parish church. The current church was constructed in 1850 and is now a Grade II listed building, providing a suitably grand backdrop for this wonderful settlement.

St Margaret's Church is thriving in Hawes

With steep hills rising to the north and the south of Hawes, it's easy to see why the Old Norse settlers gave this place the name Hals, literally meaning the pass between the hills.

The population continued to grow and it was in 1699 when King William III granted a charter for Hawes to have a weekly market on Tuesdays. If you're passing by on a Tuesday, you'll see the market still takes place. Don't expect a plethora of craft and nostalgia, though. The market itself is full of practical items that aren't necessarily sold in the local shops, and so providing a really essential service to local folk.

More interesting for the tourist is the cattle market, also held on a Tuesday. Check out the times and walk out to it, beyond the visitor centre on the main road. You'll be able to sit in the auction room and see Wensleydale farmers bid for the best sheep and cows in the area.

If you ask most people what Hawes is famous for, it's the link with Wensleydale cheese, the favourite of Wallace and Gromit. You can pay a visit to the creamery, which has a fine cheese sampling room and a great café, and it's well signed off the main road. There are fine pubs to try out in the centre of Hawes and a cracking fish and chip shop, too. Hawes has provided me with many happy memories and I can vouch for it being a great base to explore the northern Dales.

Route

Your starting point for this walk is St Margaret's Church on Main Street in Hawes; there is a car park further along the road. When you are stood looking at the church from the road, take the path that heads up the hill, signed for Gayle Lane. This path takes you around the back of the church and you then go through a gate on the left, the path then taking you across a field with Gayle Beck on the left. It's a tranquil enough stream at this point, but is the same one responsible for the waterfall you can see from the main road in Hawes and the one you'll encounter upstream on this walk.

After heading though another gate you'll come to a road, where you turn left and press on to Gayle. At the junction in Gayle, turn right and look out for the Methodist Church you'll pass on the left. Continue along this road until you leave Gayle and come to a junction; turn right here and immediately on your left you'll see the path you need. Head across a couple of fields until you come to a sign post (SD 868, 890) and should turn right following the Pennine Way. This takes you across a couple more fields and brings you to a road; turn left here and follow the road. Shortly after, take the track signed for Beggarman's Road. This is an easy track to follow, with several gates to go through and marvellous limestone walls on either side, the head of the dale in front of you providing the perfect backdrop.

Follow the track for just over 1km until you reach a metal gate on the left (grid reference SD 859, 877), where there is a path that takes you down towards the river. Before you reach the river, follow the footpath sign directing you to the left. This path takes you through a gap in the wall and then beyond a ruined building, after which you should keep to the wall on the right and go through the next gate.

Follow the side of the river, keeping on the left of it and walking beyond the footbridge. Shortly after, you reach Aysgill Force, an impressive waterfall after heavy rain. The route continues on, all the time sticking close to the river and passing through several gates. When you reach a wall and can go no further, there's a steep climb up to the left and when you're at the top you

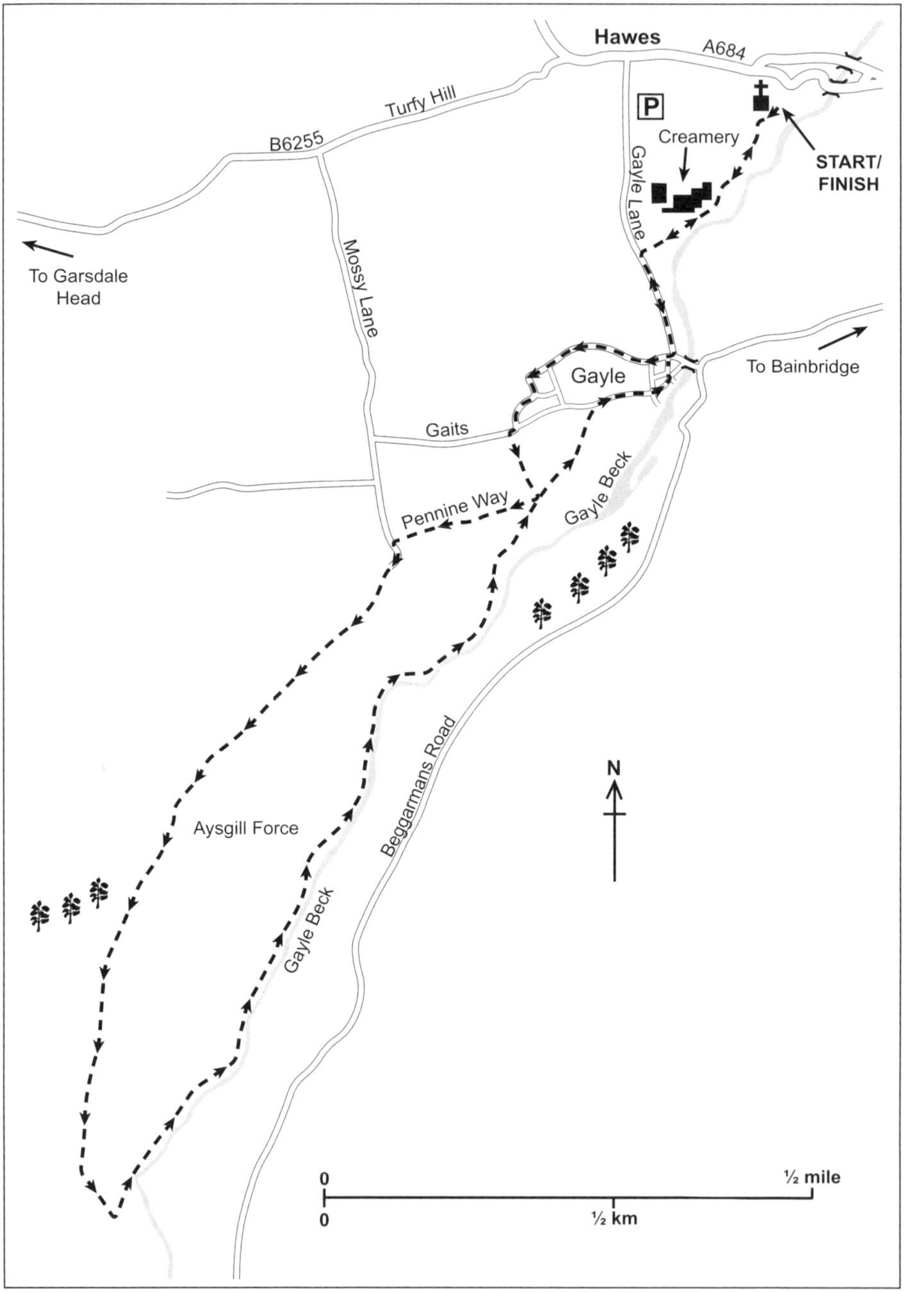

Hawes
A684
Turfy Hill
B6255
P
Creamery
START/
FINISH
Gayle Lane
To Garsdale
Head
Mossy Lane
Gayle
To Bainbridge
Gaits
Pennine Way
Gayle Beck
Aysgill Force
Beggarmans Road
Gayle Beck
N
0
½ mile
0
½ km

Some lovely remote waterfalls await you on this walk

need to go through the gate and follow the sign for Gayle. Head over the small hill and from the top you'll be able to see Gayle, the church at Hawes and the Wensleydale Creamery in the middle of both settlements.

When you get to the road, turn right and follow it until you reach the main road through Gayle, then turn left onto that and follow the sign for Hawes. Sticking to this road will take you to the creamery, and just after that there is a path off to the right that takes you diagonally over a field and brings you out at the car park in Hawes on the main street.

Rev. Kate Bottley's Thought for the Walk

Blessed are the Cheese Makers

A place can be known for many things, such as its church or famous sons and daughters. But Hawes is best known for its creamery. They've been hand making cheese in these parts for the last 100 years. The only time I've approached anything like it is when I neglected that pot of cream at the back of the fridge; it looked a bit like cottage cheese crossed with something which terrified me once on *Dr Who*. The cheese from Hawes is wholly different and so distinctive and tasty that in 2013 'Yorkshire Wensleydale' was awarded protected geographical indication by the European Union. In other words, you can only call it Yorkshire Wensleydale if it is from here. No matter how good the cheese or how closely it mimics the Hawes stuff, if it doesn't say Yorkshire Wensleydale on the label it isn't Yorkshire Wensleydale in the wrapper.

The creamery is on the site where Dairy Crest once produced their Wensleydale – but they moved production to Lancashire (the horror) in 1992 with the loss of 59 local jobs. When the new creamery rose from the ashes it was reborn stronger and more beautiful than before and now employs about 200 locals.

It must have seemed like a disaster to the community when the creamery shut and the jobs were lost. But looking back now, the creamery employs even

The waterfall in the centre of Hawes can be tame one day and thunderous the next, depending on the rain

A typical Dales scene of limestone wall and valley

more locals than ever before and it's easier to see that the closing of the dairy Crest dairy might just have been a blessing in disguise.

I don't believe, like other people sometimes say they do, that 'everything happens for a reason' or that our lives are some sort of cosmic plan determined to the last minute. Where would be the room for free will in that? But I do believe that sometimes out of desperate situations we can find opportunities we never would have believed were there.

Questions to think about along the way

What disasters have you faced in life?
Do you think everything is planned out?
How have you made the best of a bad situation?

WALK 3
Grassington

This walk by the river next to the lovely waterfalls also takes in pleasant farming country – and don't forget to pop in to the village itself, which has a great array of shops and places to get some refreshment.

What you need to know	
Distance	5.1km/3.1 miles
Time taken	2 hours
Starting point	As you follow the A6265 from Grassington towards Hebden, look out for the visitor centre. It's well signed and there is parking there. Grid reference SE 002, 637
Difficulty	A gentle stroll by the river and across farmland
Refreshments	The Cobblestones Café in Grassington has a good reputation and is a good place to stop for a rest, though if it's busy there are other options in the village to settle down in as well. Tel: 01756 752303 Postcode: BD23 5AQ
Map	OS Explorer OL2: Yorkshire Dales South and Western Area

Grassington

With its cobbled streets and quaint shops, this is one of the best villages in the Dales to explore and you should plan to spend some of your day investigating the centre as you walk through it. But take time to plan what time of the year to go to Grassington if you like taking part in festivals as there are a couple of great ones to attend. In the summer there is a two-week long festival of music and performance to indulge in, while the autumn sees a 1940s festival take place and winter is the time when a Dickensian festival is put on. But there are things to see and do here all year round, not least the small folk museum that you'll find in an old lead miner's cottage. If you find yourself thinking that some of the scenes in this area are familiar, it may be because you've seen them on the big screen. The original *Calendar Girls* came from villages just to the south of Grassington and plenty of places around Grassington were used when making the film.

As you set out on the walk, you'll soon come to Linton Falls and there is a lot of historic significance here. When you pass the falls, spare a thought for how important they have been for bringing power to the village. In 1909 a forward-thinking hydro-electric turbine was installed that brought early electricity to Grassington until the village was connected to the National Grid. In 2012 the same turbine house was used to install a new turbine, producing 500,000 kwh per year.

Linton Falls – Power to the people

Route

Park up in the National Park Visitor Centre, which is well signed as you enter Grassington and found at grid reference SE 002, 637. From the car park, make

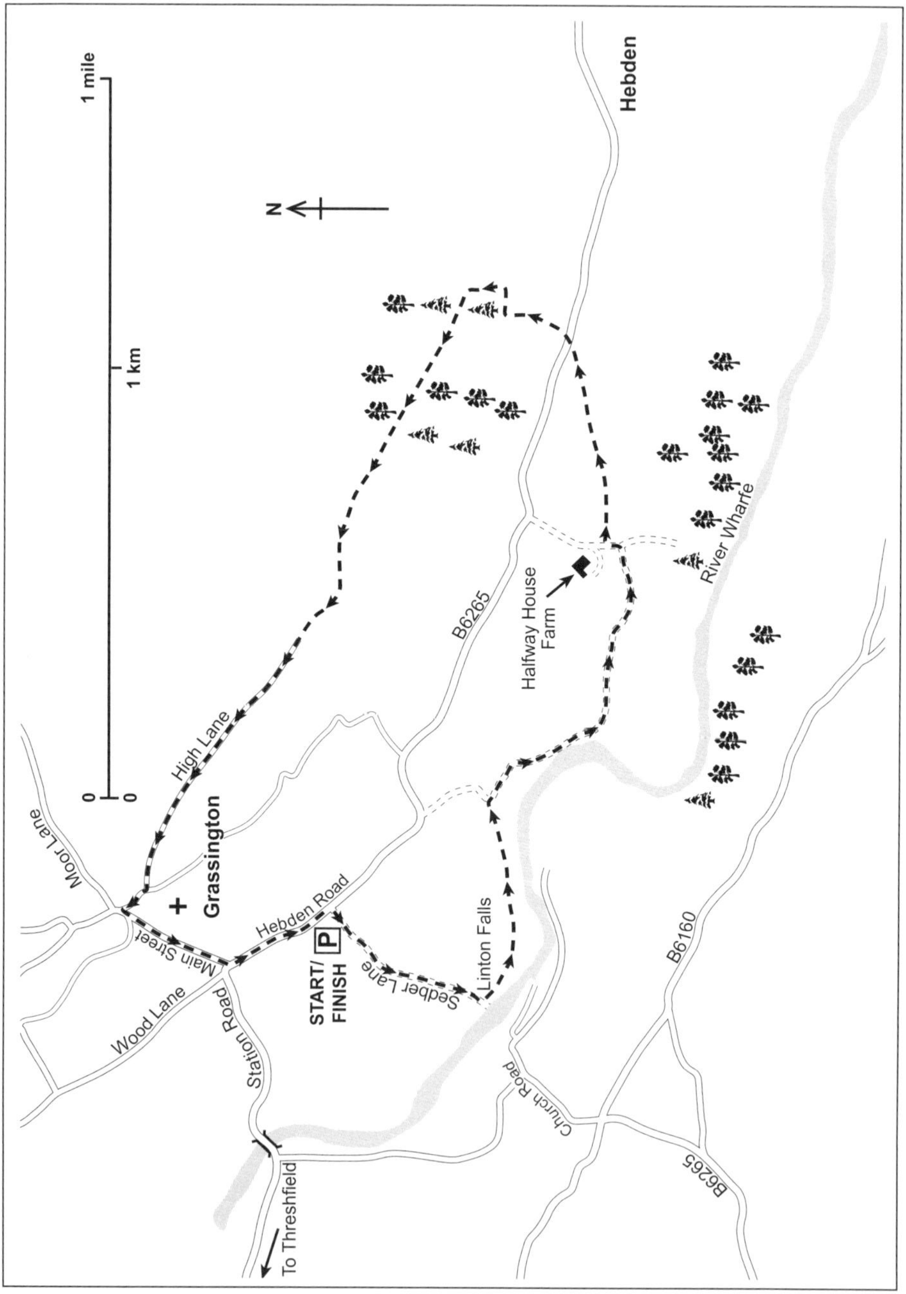
1 mile
1 km
0
0
N
Hebden
B6265
Halfway House Farm
River Wharfe
High Lane
Grassington
Moor Lane
Hebden Road
Main Street
START/ FINISH
P
Sedber Lane
Linton Falls
Wood Lane
Station Road
To Threshfield
Church Road
B6160
B6265

your way away from the road to the bottom left corner of the car park and pass through the gate onto Sedber Lane.

You'll approach Linton Falls, a really impressive sight, and you should stay on this side of the river and turn left along the path. Cross a couple of fields on an easy to follow path and you'll come to a small lane, where you need to turn right. Pass by some buildings and cross a field, and when you go over the wall look out for the path ahead, turning left onto it. The track turns to the left and then you need to watch out for a path on the right. This forks in two beyond the first wall and you follow the path that goes to the left (grid reference SE 012, 631).

Follow this path as it makes its way across fields and up to the B6265. Cross the road and continue along the path at the other side, this path soon enters a wood. In the middle of the wood, look out for the path that turns to the left and take it, leaving the wood and crossing a series of fields on a well-signed route. This path, passing other wooded areas and crossing fields, will

There's no other way – follow the well-marked route

This charming village – Grassington has a lot of appeal

eventually lead you to a track known as High Lane. This lane will bring you out in Grassington and a left turn will take you past the church.

Grassington is a charming village, full of great places to shop and eat. Have a meander around the shops on the road that leads down the hill. When you get to the bottom, turn left on the road and continue on here until you reach the Visitor Centre, which you'll see on your right.

Rev. Kate Bottley's Thought for the Walk

Time team

Wander through Grassington at a certain time of year and you'll be forgiven for thinking you've slipped through the time frame continuum into a different era all together. The town loves its time travel and every September it hosts a 1940s weekend. People travel from miles around dressed up as land girls, GIs and ARP wardens so they can dance to big bands and indulge in a bit of harmless nostalgia. In winter the town gets dressed up again for the annual Dickensian festival, where you can eat pork pies with Little Dorrit and stick you head round the door on Miss Haversham. It's all good fun and loved by many.

Nostalgia for time gone past is a harmless pursuit many enjoy. And the conversation often includes the phrase 'the good old days.' My Gran (God rest her) was a little less sentimental about the olden days. Before she died at the ripe age of 101 and before dementia had taken the best of her, she would often baulk at the phrase 'the good old days'. 'Rationing and scarlet fever, hardly good!' The Dickensian era (although my Gran didn't witness that) was not all smart top hats and crinolines either. There was high infant mortality, little proper sanitation and poor health care.

Nostalgia for the past is all well and good but counting the blessing of the present is more important, I think. What if the best days of our lives are the ones we are living in now?

Questions to think about along the way

If you could travel back to an historical era when would it be and why?
When were the 'good old days'?
What's the best thing about modern life?

WALK 4
Keld

Some great waterfalls are to be found at this junction of long distance routes, where the Pennine Way crosses the Coast to Coast path.

What you need to know	
Distance	9.5 km/5.9 miles
Time taken	3 hours 30 minutes
Starting point	There are some steep climbs on this well signed route. Starting point: Keld is to be found on the B6270, just to the north of Thwaite. Turn off the main road and head down into the village. There's a car park at the camp site. Grid reference NY 891, 012
Difficulty	There are some steep climbs on this well signed route
Refreshments	For refreshments, stop off in Muker when you're finished to find the Farmer's Arms. Telephone: 01748 886297 www.farmersarmsmuker.co.uk Postcode: DL11 6QG
Map	OS Explorer OL30: Yorkshire Dales North and Central Area

Keld

A lot of the walkers passing through Keld may be wearier than you are. The village has the unique feature of being the point where the Coast to Coast path meets the Pennine Way, so there may be a few backpackers a fair way along with their personal challenge to complete an iconic long distance trek. Some of them will have left Edale in the Peak District a few days ago, on their way up to the Scottish borders. Others will have stepped out from St Bees in Cumbria, heading east to the North Sea.

As you walk through Keld today, you may not see any local folk going about their business; it's certainly hard to imagine this being a thriving village home

Another brick in the wall – keep an eye out for fossils in the limestone

to 6,000 people. But that's certainly what Keld used to be like, back in the late 19th century when the place was thriving on the local lead-mining industry. It was at this time of growth and development that the facilities in Keld expanded; two chapels were built alongside a school and literary institute.

Today, there is no shop and the only businesses - a campsite and youth hostel - are there to look after the passing trade stomping by in walking boots and usually staying one night. But this is a place that deserves exploration even if you're not on a longer trek like the Pennine Way.

Keld is built close to a limestone gorge, meaning there are waterfalls in the area well worth looking at - especially after periods of heavy rain. Several of them can be seen on this walk, giving you yet another sample of the wonderful scenery to be enjoyed in the Yorkshire Dales.

Route

Keld is a small settlement north of Swaledale that gets plenty of walkers passing close by because it's a convenient stop on the Pennine Way and the

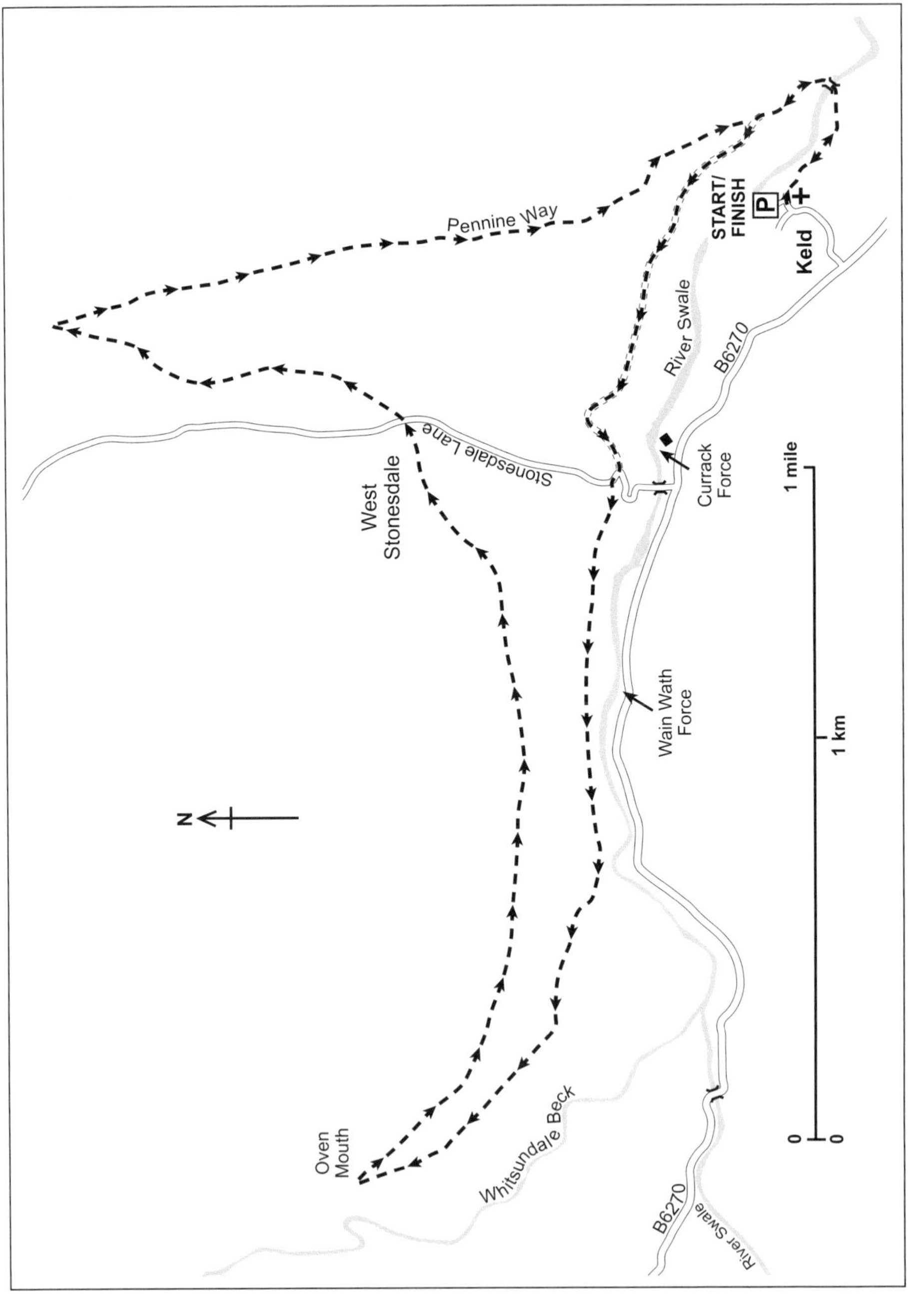

Pennine Way
START/
FINISH
P
Keld
River Swale
B6270
Stonesdale Lane
West
Stonesdale
Currack
Force
Wain Wath
Force
N
1 mile
1 km
0
0
Oven
Mouth
Whitsundale Beck
B6270
River Swale

Coast to Coast walk. Turn off the B6270 when it's signed for Keld and at the bottom of the hill you'll see a car park you can use that is part of a farm's campsite.

From the car park, head back to the road and you'll see the church on the right. The walk heads along the bridleway that is signed as the Coast to Coast walk. Carry on down the hill and at the junction turn left, following signs for the Pennine Way and continue across the bridge. You'll now be able to see the first waterfall of the walk, Catrake Force tumbling away on the right.

Go straight ahead when you have crossed the bridge, and when you come to a signpost make sure you turn left and head along the Pennine Way. There's now a steep climb that brings you to a house, where you turn left and follow the public bridleway. This is an easy track to follow, giving good views down into the valley on your left. You'll go down into a dip and pass Currack Falls before climbing up the track on the other side.

At the top, go through the gate and cross the road, picking up the path again on the other side. Heading along this path and passing the fields, keep an eye

Carrying on through it all, the waterfalls provide a never-ending spectacle on the walk

out for the river down on the left, where you'll be able to see Wath Wain Falls. The drop away to the left gets very steep as you make your way across Cotterby Scar.

Passing some wooded areas and going through gates, the path climbs up and brings you to a track. Turn right here (grid reference NY 876, 016) and continue on up, passing an old ruined house and another abandoned building.

As you continue to follow this path, you'll eventually start to climb up and you'll see a wooden pole you should head towards (NY 868, 022); this Coast to Coast marker is the place where you need to turn right and begin the trek up the hill. This grassy path almost turns back on yourself and one of the first things you can see on the right are the ruined buildings you went by earlier. The path over this grassy pasture can be tricky to follow at times but the key for this section of the walk is to stick fairly close to the wall you can see on the right; as long as you don't lose sight of this you'll be fine.

As you get towards the small settlement of West Stonedale, you'll enter a valley and should stick to the right hand side of this as you proceed down to the road. Turn left on the road and look out for the footpath on the right as the road bends away. Follow the footpath signs over the fields and cross the footbridge. Turn left at the other side and follow the path close to the river as you make your way up Stonesdale. You'll see another footbridge crossing the river, but instead of crossing it you need to follow the path as it bends off to the right and heads towards a building.

On the top of the world, looking down on Stonesdale

Climb up along the path and aim for the wall at the top, where a stile will allow you to reach the other side (grid reference NY 889, 028). Turn left and follow the path up the hill, but after a few metres you'll reach a substantial track; this is the Pennine Way and you need to turn right onto it.

After going through a couple of gates, the track starts to slowly descend and you'll come to an old farm building, where you follow the Pennine Way sign to the right. Follow the track with two dry stone walls on either side and when you reach the farm, turn right and follow the Pennine Way again beyond the waterfall. Cross the footbridge and when you reach the track, turn right towards Keld to complete the walk.

Rev. Kate Bottley's Thought for the Walk

Come apart and rest a while (or you might just come apart)

I have a favourite jumper. It started out life as my training hoody for when I played ladies rugby. I'd put it on at the end of a training session to keep me warm. It got covered in mud, some of which I still can't get out. When I went out as a student, clubbing in Leeds city centre, the jumper came with me. It spent some of its life on the dance floor being danced round and trodden on. When I bought my first home I wore it for decorating. I wore it in hospital when the kids were born, wore it snowballing and wore it out walking. The jumper has seen better days. Its paint splattered, muddy and stained and it's also, after 25 years of wear, pretty holey too.

It has a different kind of holiness, though: a holiness of experience. But it's tired and it needs a rest.

The Keld Resource Centre has spent time in Keld repairing and rebuilding the buildings at the heart of the community, also establishing a 'Well-being garden' as a place for anyone and everyone to take time to repair and rebuild themselves.

We can become stained and stressed by life, over used, over worked and starting to show signs of wear and tear. The 'stains' we bear are ones which show the wonderful story of our lives, but even the holiest of people need time to rest and to re-create.

My jumper has a few patches on it now, but I'll keep wearing it and repairing it.

Questions to think about along the way:

How do you relax?
What scars and stains do you carry with you?
Where is your place of refreshment and relaxation?
If you could change anything about your past what would it be?

WALK 5
Masham

The market town of Masham makes a great day out, both for visiting the church and supplementing your trip with a brewery tour. This walk lets you experience some of the surrounding countryside.

What you need to know	
Distance	8km/5 miles
Time taken	2 hours
Starting point	Park in the main square, close to the church. Grid reference SD 226, 807
Difficulty	Some paths near the river can be very muddy after wet weather, otherwise this is a gently walk without steep climbs
Refreshments	You're spoilt for choice for pubs in Masham, but a good choice is the White Bear Hotel. Tel: 01765 689319. www.thewhitebearhotel.co.uk Postcode: HG4 4EN
Map	OS Explorer 302: Northallerton & Thirsk

Masham

First, the golden rule: you've got to be able to pronounce the name of this place correctly. It's the centre of a thriving real ale industry and if you can't get the name right you'll stick out like a pint of lager shandy. So, whatever you do, don't arrive here and start calling it 'Mash-em'. It's not pronounced as you might think. Instead, forget the 'h' is in there and call it 'Mass'm'. Then you'll have less chance of being the black sheep of the village.

Although the town is dominated by the large market square that is home to many stalls on Wednesdays and Saturdays, the clue to the main reason people

The outstanding church in the centre of Masham

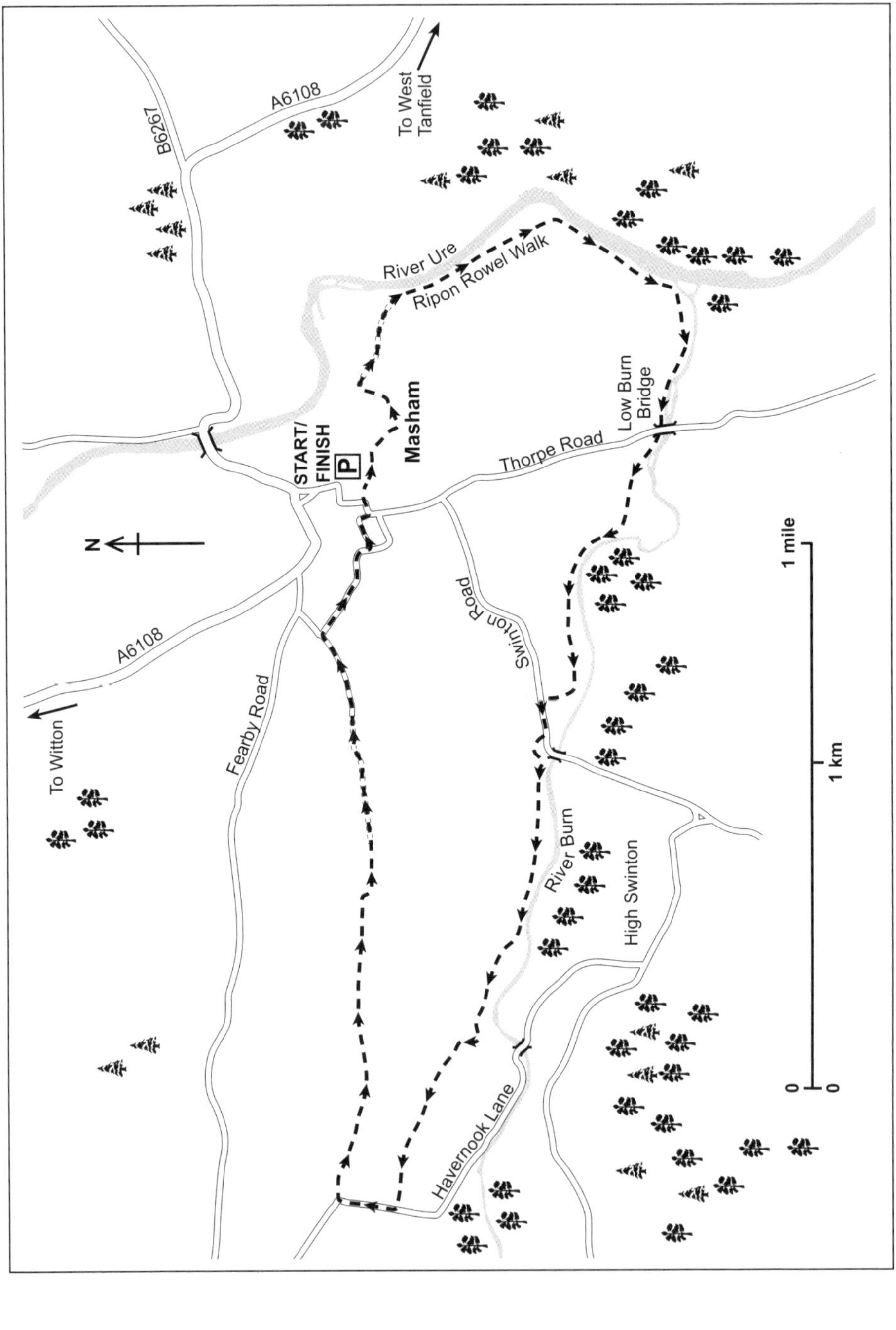

B6267
A6108
To West Tanfield
River Ure
Ripon Rowel Walk
Masham
START/ FINISH
P
Low Burn Bridge
Thorpe Road
N
Swinton Road
A6108
Fearby Road
To Witton
River Burn
High Swinton
Haverock Lane
1 mile
1 km
0
0

visit can first be savoured by the smell of hops that drifts over the whole settlement. There are two nationally important breweries here, neither far from the main square but both hidden among the back streets. The oldest of the two is Theakston's, makers of the great Old Peculiar ale, and there's a good tour to be had there. Be sure also to check out their flagship pub, The White Bear, which serves wonderful food and drink, standing imposingly right next to the rival Black Sheep brewery. This brewery, too, has a smashing tour as well as a bistro and plenty of opportunity to buy souvenirs. There's a great family story that goes with the two breweries being in the same town and it stems back to 1992, when Paul Theakston disagreed with the family's decision to sell off the brewery. He decided to set his own brewery up and hence the name Black Sheep.

The church which features in this walk, St Mary's, is found just off the main square and is worth exploring, either at the start of the walk when you pass it or to pass some of the afternoon after your stroll. There are monuments inside for two wealthy families who occupied local country houses and near the doorway you'll find an early 9th century Saxon shaft with detailed carvings.

Route

Park in the main square, where there is an honesty box. From here, you can see the church towering up in the corner. Head over to that corner and go into the church grounds. Walk down by the side of the church and continue straight ahead, heading through the gate and joining the footpath on the other side.

Turn left and head over the grass, passing through another gate and heading down the hill. Passing another gate at the bottom and then turning right onto a track, this takes you by a house on the right and you continue to follow this track. This is an easy to follow track, and you'll soon see the river on your left and crops in a farming field on your right. The river bends to the right, slowing for a while but then picking up speed again. After a while, the path bends round to the right and you start to follow a tributary of the river; look out for a path on the left that takes you down some steps and to the water's edge.

The route follows the river and will bring you to a road where you need to carefully cross and pick it up again at the other side. You walk across fields here, again with the river on the left and with signs making it easy to follow. Over a wooden footbridge, the path takes you once again to the side of the water, then away from it into fields. Coming to another road, turn left onto it and follow the path on the right that takes you into a golf course. Head for the club house and turn left after it, following the yellow arrows that take you back to the river.

After following this path for a while and staying on the right hand side of the water, you'll find yourself coming back onto the golf course; follow the signs as it directs you to leave the course via a gate on the left. Follow this track and it will eventually bring you out at a road, where you need to turn right. Climb the hill until the road bends to the left and there is a track going straight ahead; at this point, take the path on the right across farmland. Halfway through the first field the path bends away to the right and you go through a gap in the wall to the second field. You can see the spire of the church ahead, giving you a point to aim for.

The walk will take you to the bridge

Take a brewery tour while you are in the village

Continue ahead, bending round to the right by the trees at the bottom of the field and then turning left to head through another field. You come out at a large animal feed works; go past it and then turn right onto Westholme Lee Road. You'll pass the Theakstones brewery and a fire station and should follow this road around to the left. Turning left at the junction, you'll be heading for the main square in Masham once more.

Rev. Kate Bottley's Thought for the Walk

Family Ties

Every family has something. Every funeral visit I do, every conversation with a wedding couple, it doesn't take long before someone at the gathering says "There's really something we should tell you vicar...". And then the stories begin, a family falling out or a feud, the cause of which is long forgotten but the ripples of which are well and truly still felt. I have to remember of course be it wedding, christening or funeral that Auntie So and So really mustn't sit anywhere near Cousin Whatdoyoucallhim and whatever you do don't mention that New Year's Eve party where Uncle Whatshisface insulted Grandad. At the first funeral I ever did as a fresh faced curate, there was a fight.

No family is exempt (even my own). From Princes to Paupers, every family has its own story. The Theakston family of Masham fame are the same, with family and board falling out and Paul Theakston eventually leaving and setting up his own Black Sheep brewery.

Families fall out. Friends argue. From Jesus' disciples to the Royal family, no one is exempt from broken human relationships. We are human, we mess up.

Some of the arguments we have with friends and family are easily repaired. Others will never be fixed and no amount of rending garments will change it. We can choose to ignore the effect these fall outs have on us or we can, wisely I think, reflect on them and use them to shape our lives in the future. The scars we bear help form us into better people.

Questions to think about along the way

What's your family like?

Are there painful relationships in your own family?

Are you the black sheep? Or is someone else?

WALK 6
Glasshouses

Follow a section of the Six Dales Trail as you enjoy a lovely walk from this pleasant village.

What you need to know	
Distance	9.5km/5.9 miles
Time taken	3 hours
Starting point	Park on the road close to the church. Grid reference SD 173, 645
Difficulty	There are some steep sections along paths that are well signed
Refreshments	Head to nearby Pately Bridge after the walk and try the Bridge Inn, on Low Wath Road. Tel: 01423 711484. Postcode: HG3 5HL
Map	OS Explorer 298: Nidderdale

Glasshouses

Often overlooked at the expense of more famous tourist haunts in the surrounding dales, Glasshouses has some lovely countryside and is worth investing a day to explore. You'll find it not far from Pately Bridge on the eastern edge of Nidderdale. Indeed, it is the River Nidd that explains the location of this small village as a twine mill was established on the river banks, using the water as a source of power. Today, the mill building is still standing (although without the original chimney) and is home to a few local businesses that you'll pass near the end of the walk.

Route

From the church on the main road running through Glasshouses, follow the road down the hill. Stick to this road as it takes you by a school on the right and then over Glasshouses bridge where you'll see the River Nidd flowing beneath you. After the bridge, the road bends off to the right and you should take the track that heads to the left. Pass the house and then take the track that goes to the right immediately after. Go past the cottages and continue along the track as it enters a wood.

You're following the route of the Six Dales Trail at this point and should keep to the main path as it climbs through the woods, with the landscape becoming rockier as you climb. When you've done the main climb, the path levels off and makes for a nice stroll through the woods; when you emerge from the trees, look out for a gate on the left and follow the signed path through there, finding a track fenced in on both sides. Go through a couple of fields and then go through a gate bringing you out to another field, where you go straight across towards the trees.

Keep crossing the fields and following the path; you'll soon come to a small river that you need to use stones to cross (grid reference SE 177, 626). Climbing up the other side, head for the top of the field. You've now got several fields to cross on your way to Northwoods Barn and you should keep an eye out for the white arrow signs that have

People in Glasshouses enjoy wonderful countryside in their local area

You'll pass two churches on this walk, with this second one in Dacre Banks

been painted onto rocks on the wall. Having walked beyond the house, you'll come onto track that is easy to follow. When this track reaches a junction with Monk Ing Road, turn left and head down on another track. At the bottom, when the track bends to the left (grid reference SE 184, 616), you need to take the path on the right and follow the Nidderdale Way.

The signage here get a little vague; you should head for the far right of the first field. When you move into the next field, turn right and head for the

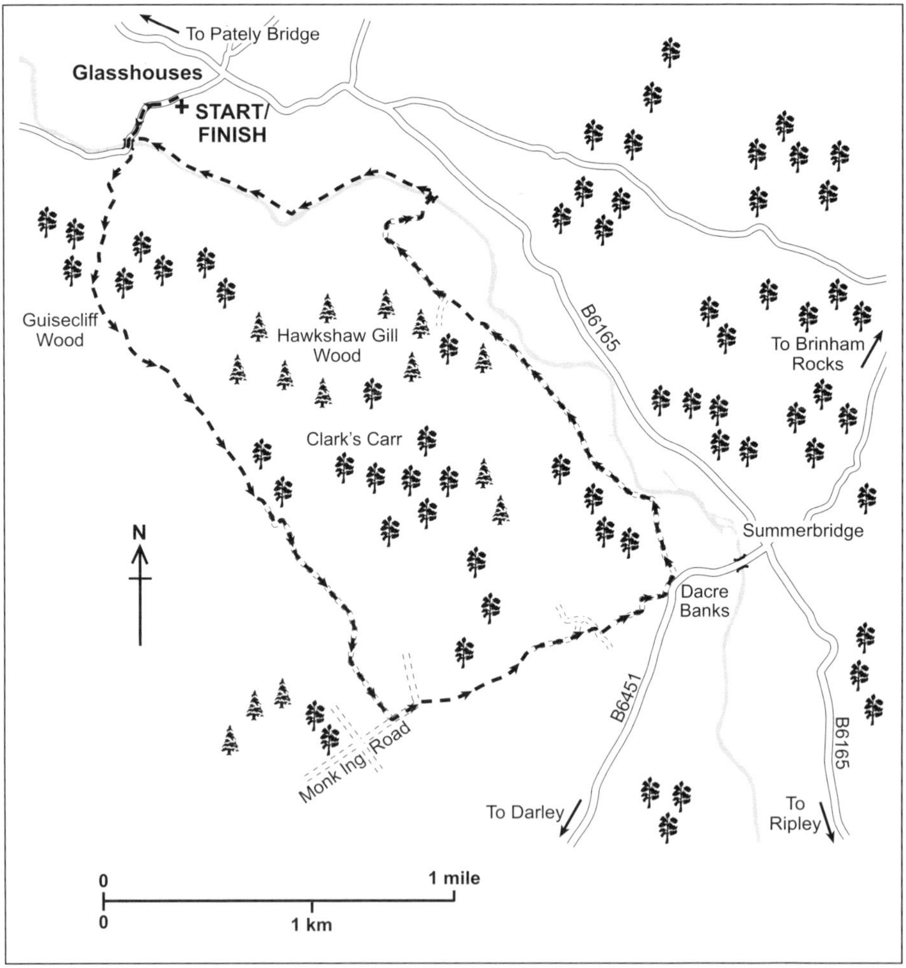

corner of the field. Then turn left and follow the wall down to the bottom, aiming for the far right side of the field. Follow the path through the next field as it heads for a farm and, once there, pick up the track that takes you further down, bending off to the right. Before you reach the next set of houses, look out for the path that leads away to the left (grid reference SE 193, 619).

This path takes you down into Dacre Banks and will bring you out onto a road; follow this as it turns first to the left and then to the right. Just before this road brings you to the main B6451 road, take the track that leads away to the left called Harewell Lane. You'll pass another church on your right and also signs to the left of an old dismantled railway. Follow the path further and you'll actually cross over the former track, leaving the embankment now on your right. This track is easy to follow and for much of the time runs parallel to the old track, but when you come to a house called Valley View you should take the path after it that heads down to the river on the right. Turn left at the bottom of the steps and you'll find yourself walking on the left of

Find the river on your right as you walk back to Glasshouses

the river, with the water flowing towards you. The path can get a little rocky here and there may be the need to use stepping stones, but continue ahead until you reach the footbridge (SE 185, 640) and then turn right across it.

Spring is in the air!

At the other side of the bridge, turn left and follow the riverside path over a stream and under the remains of the old railway bridge. The path then follows the river for almost the entire route back, save for a section that crosses a field. You're brought out at buildings that house a garage amongst other businesses; follow the road around the building and you'll reach the main road through Glasshouses. Turn right and climb up the hill to reach the church once again.

Rev. Kate Bottley's Thought for the Walk

A rope of three cords is not easily broken

Glasshouses is neither a big nor a particular spectacular place. It doesn't boast internationally renowned cheese or world class breweries. Glasshouses doesn't have a theme park. It has its church, of course, and its pub. But there's not much that differentiates this from other North Yorkshire villages. It's pretty and pleasant but relativity unremarkable. It's humble, ordinary and steady. It enjoys a great May Day celebration with dancing round the maypole on the village green but it's quiet and pleasant. A peaceful sort of place. A sort of 'nothing much to see here' sort of place. Beautiful, but not bold or flashy.

In its history Glasshouses was the site of an Old Twine mill on the banks of the Nidd. Presumably it was the site of some glass houses at some point too. Twine doesn't have the grandeur of rope or the delicacy of thread, it's not pretty like ribbon or posh like silk. Twine is used for tying up plants and for marking out straight lines and despite its ordinariness, it is what it is and it's good at its job. Twine isn't hauling ships into port or helping designers make beautiful couture. Twine could be called boring.

A wise friend once said to me "Bloom where you are planted". Some people lead amazing, grand and exciting lives and never even leave their front porch. Others have the dullest of existences while drinking the finest champagne and sleeping in the grandest hotels. We may aspire for a better life but the best one might be right here.

There is much to be said for the ordinary, the usual, and the practical. While twine might not have built an empire, it kept the allotment tidy and the pantry full. Twine might lie forgotten in the junk drawer from time to time but when you need it, it's reliable, steady and sure.

There's plenty to be said for humble and honest.

Questions to think about along the way

Is your life ordinary or extra ordinary?
What is an ordinary day like for you?
How many different types of rope/twine can you name and their uses?

WALK 7
Gargrave

Get a glimpse of life by the Leeds-Liverpool Canal on this lovely countryside stroll.

What you need to know	
Distance	10km/6.2 miles
Time taken	3 hours 30 minutes
Starting point	Gargrave is easily reached on the A65, north of Skipton. From the main road, take the road over the bridge towards Broughton and park near the church. Grid reference SD 931, 539
Difficulty	Paths may be muddy after wet weather. Some gentle climbs
Refreshments	On the main road in Gargrave you'll see the Dalesman Café, which is worth popping in for a drink and snack. Tel: 01756 749250 Postcode: BD23 3LX
Map	OS Explorer OL2: Yorkshire Dales South and Western Area

Gargrave

You have to press on out of Skipton for four miles before you reach this decent-sized village. When compared to the bright lights and big attractions of its nearby town, on the face of it there doesn't seem to be much going on in Gargrave and the number of visitors you'll see will certainly reflect that. Sure, there are a few good pubs and a couple of cosy tea rooms that can quench your thirst or satisfy your hunger. But you need to look away from the village boundary to find the best reason to base your walk in Gargrave.

The walks from here are simply stunning, it being at the heart of the rolling dales and cattle country that make this National Park so famous. And, as you'll discover on this stroll, one of the gems that Gargrave has to offer is its proximity to the canal that winds from Leeds to Liverpool; the engineers had to negotiate a tricky climb near Gargrave and so there are several locks for you to see on your way.

St Andrew's Church

The church, of course, is the focal point for this walk, and unsurprisingly for a building dedicated to St Andrew you're likely to find the Scottish flag flying outside. It's an attractive church, and one full of history. Note that the brick of the tower is a slightly different colour to the rest of the building. This is because it is the original tower still standing from when it was built using stone from a Roman villa around 1521, while the rest of the church was rebuilt with stone from a different source in 1852. The church is open each day until dusk and you are welcome to go in and explore some of the wonderful features inside. One of the most notable is the large amount of stained glass to be found in this church, including some pieces made by the renowned Capronnier of Brussels. Look out also for the Anglo-Danish crosses that date back to the tenth century.

The entrance to the church

Gargrave, then, is a village of contrasts, blending the new with the old, the busy trunk road through the middle with the deserted paths a few minutes out of the village. But despite the rumble of trucks pressing on down the main road, this is still a cracking place to live.

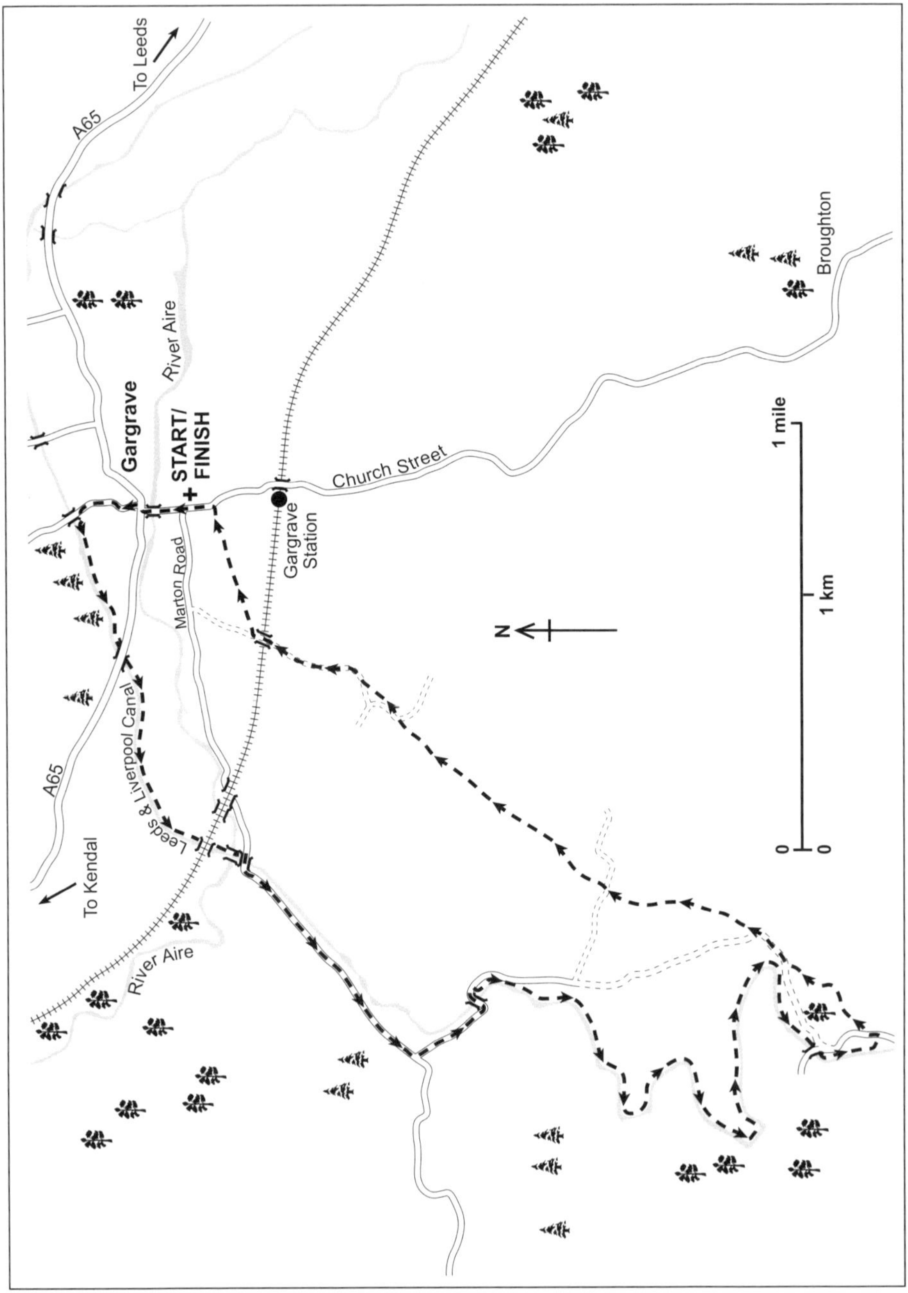

To Leeds
A65
Gargrave
River Aire
START/
FINISH
Church Street
Gargrave
Station
Marton Road
Broughton
N
1 mile
1 km
0
0
Leeds & Liverpool Canal
A65
To Kendal
River Aire

Route

Starting from St Andrew's Church at grid reference SD 931, 539, head into Gargrave, crossing over the River Aire and reaching the main road that cuts through village. Cross over and take the road that goes straight ahead at the other side, to the right of the café. Follow this road as it bends right then left and follow the sign for the canal.

When you reach the canal, turn left onto the towpath and follow the sign pointing towards Blackburn and Liverpool (grid reference SD 931, 543). The journey along the canal will take you out of Gargrave and under a bridge that carries the A65 overhead.

The first of several locks is found immediately after, number 33 on this canal called Anchor Lock. You'll see a pub on the left and should keep to the canal as you pass lock 34, Scarland Lock. This is a nice stretch, with farming fields all around and the train line coming into sight on the left. Go under bridge 169 and you'll see another lock straight after, then it's not long until you pass under the railway line via bridge 168.

The canal passes over a river, then the path leaves the canal side and brings you to a road; cross over the bridge and follow the road as it heads by the canal, before picking up the towpath again when you get chance thanks to a gate on the left.

You're now coming up to Bank Newton Locks, a lovely part of the route when the canal deals with the change in gradient by having a quick succession of locks and holding areas for barges waiting. The first one is called Bottom Lock and you walk beyond the rest of them and pass the old canal side houses.

The path leaves the canal once more and takes you to the road, where you again cross over the canal and stick to the road before picking up the towpath once more; this time you'll be on the left of the canal as you walk.

The towpath is a lovely place to walk

The next section of the canal route is interesting as the canal is clearly built up on an embankment, a little like you're perhaps more used to seeing train lines. It bends around and goes over Nuttleber Dike. You can see Langber TV mast on the left, but as the canal once again bends around, this ends up being on your right as you pass it. Follow the bending canal some more, but when you reach bridge 163 at Green Bank you take the path off to the left. Head down the hill here, turning left soon after and following the track through Langber Plantation. Follow this track straight ahead and follow the Pennine Way signs, but when the track bends to the left you need to take the Pennine Way off to the right at SD 914, 517. Go through the gate and up the hill, over the footbridge at the top.

The Leeds-Liverpool canal cuts through the countryside

Follow the Pennine Way signs across the fields and cross the track at Newton Grange Farm. Continue crossing the fields and following the well-place signs until you reach a signpost at a crossroads (grid reference SD 922, 531). Go straight ahead on the Pennine Way, with the path turning into a track and crossing the railway. Immediately after the bridge, take the Pennine Way path on the right and cross the fields that will lead you into Gargrave. Pass the houses at the end of the final field and come to the road, where you turn left. You'll soon find yourself back at the church you set out from.

Rev. Kate Bottley's Thought for the Walk

Gargrave is a beautiful place to visit at any time of the year and the church of Saint Andrew's is charming. The pubs are pleasant and the surrounding landscape stunning. On your walk today you'll have discovered a beautiful gem of the British countryside. But with the utmost respect to Gargrave, it's not the church, the pub or even the view that's my favourite part of the village.

That honour goes to something a little humbler and more ordinary. I love the stepping stones across the river. I've always loved stepping stones. Where I grew up in Sheffield there are some marvellous stones across the River Rivelin, built from bits of an old water mill that used to stand proudly on the bank side. When I was little it seemed like each one was a mile apart and I'd worry my little legs wouldn't get me across. To be honest at, 5 foot 1 inch I'm still not totally convinced even now. I'll confess that once or twice, even as a grown up, I've mistimed the steps on the crossing and gone home with a soggy sock. But the risk of getting wet was always worth taking for the fun of crossing the stepping stones. Of course stepping stones are a practical way to get across the river which doesn't have a bridge but there are many times when we use the stepping stones not through necessity but just for the fun of it.

We often take necessary risks in our lives, stepping out onto a path that we don't know will lead to success or failure. But sometimes we might need to take risks not because we have to but just for the fun of it. Just to feel the pulse pound, the adrenaline rush and to feel alive. It's the thing that makes people bungee jump, roller blade and eat fire. Well calculated risk can be a scary sort of fun. And while crossing the stones at Gargrave is not quite the same as bungee jumping, the chance that you might mistime the step and end up in the river is half the fun of it in the first place. And of course a stepping stone is always just a place to put your feet before the next step of faith on the journey.

Questions to think about along the way

What's the biggest adrenaline rush you've ever had?

When have you mistimed your step and ended up making an error of judgement?

What have the stepping stones in your own life lead you on to?

WALK 8
Bolton Abbey

Visually stunning and steeped in history, the walk from Bolton Abbey up the River Nidd is one to cherish - as are the cakes in the tea room!

What you need to know	
Distance	12km/7.4 miles
Time taken	4 hours
Starting point	The pay and display car park at Bolton Abbey. Grid reference SE 071, 539
Difficulty	There are some steep sections, but this is a well-used route with well-maintained paths
Refreshments	On the way up the river and on the way back, you will pass the Cavendish Pavilion Café within the Bolton Abbey Estate. Tel: 01756 710245 www.cavendishpavilion.co.uk Postcode: BD23 6AN
Map	OS Explorer OL2: Yorkshire Dales South and Western Area

Bolton Abbey

Sitting just inside the Yorkshire Dales National Park, the Bolton Abbey estate - owned by the Cavendish family who live at Chatsworth House - is one of the top destinations in the region and has developed facilities to match.

The priory was founded in 1154 by the Augustinian order and survived until the early 14th century, when Scottish raiders led to it being abandoned and caused structural damage. Building work at Bolton Abbey was still ongoing when the Dissolution of the Monasteries in 1540 signalled an end to the construction. The east end remains in ruins to this day, although work was added to the remaining church in Victorian days and it is still a working priory today.

Abbey Road: This amazing sight is just off the B6160

The Bolton Abbey estate as a whole is spread over 33,000 acres and there are six Sites of Special Scientific Interest within it, the most significant of these being the ancient oak woodland and section of the River Wharfe called The Strid. Photographers still flock to Bolton Priory to capture the surreal beauty of a ruined building in wonderful surroundings. Turner captured it in watercolours during 1809 and the work of art entitled *Bolton Abbey, Yorkshire*, is kept at the British Museum.

Route

From the main car park at Bolton Abbey, head past the main toilet block and get to the road. Turn left onto the road and then go through the gap in the wall you'll see on the right. Go through the gate and down the steps, towards the priory. You'll now go over a small stream and beyond the abbey, taking the footbridge across the river on the right. You can take the stepping stones if you're feeling brave, although after heavy rain they can become a bit too dodgy!

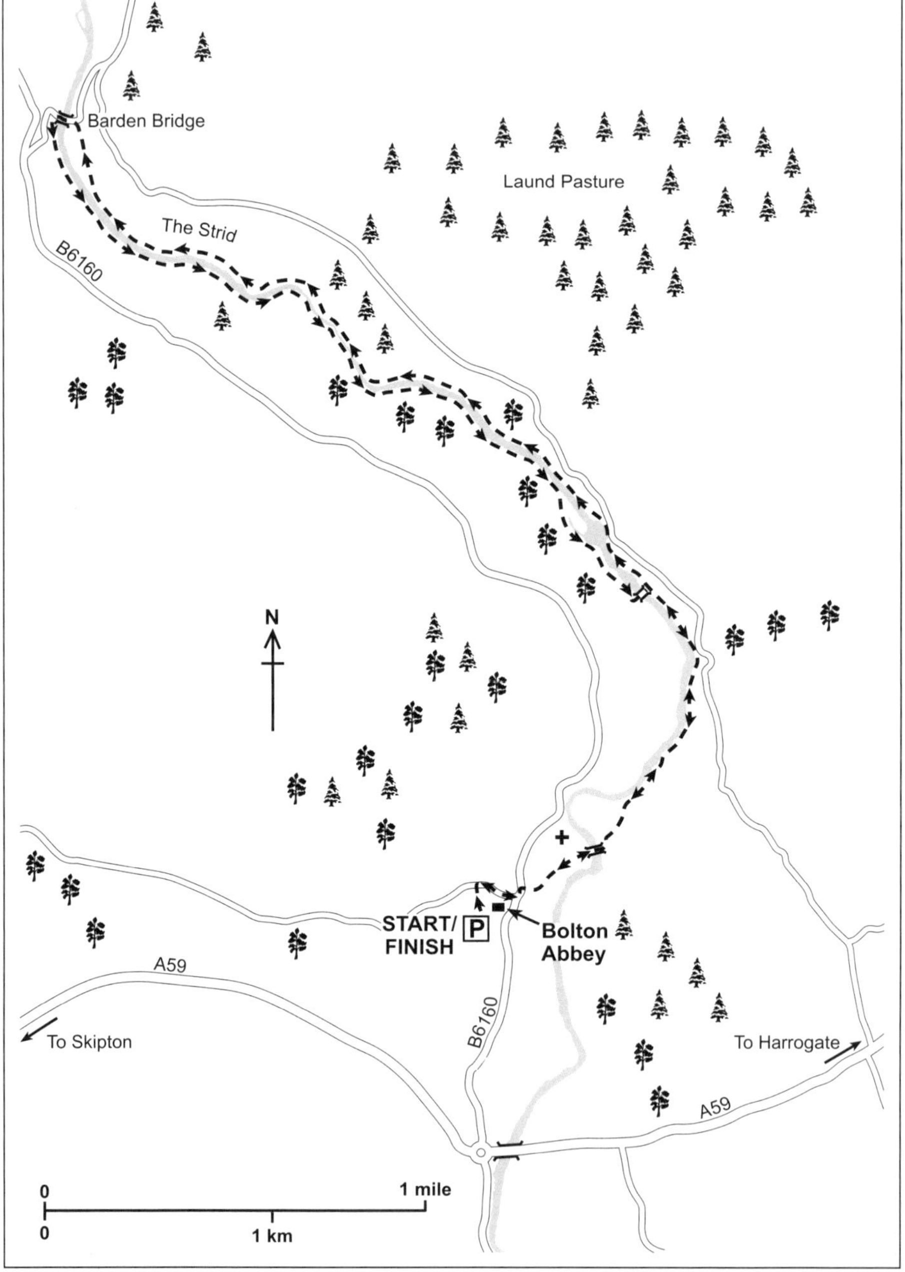
Barden Bridge
Laund Pasture
The Strid
B6160
N
START/
FINISH
P
Bolton
Abbey
A59
To Skipton
B6160
To Harrogate
A59
0
1 mile
0
1 km

At the other side, take the riverside path and go through a gate and down into a dip, with the river still on your left. You get brought out at a road (SE 080, 545), where you need to turn left and cross the ford before taking the footpath on the left. Continue on this path, passing the café on the other side of the river and sticking to path as it follows the river on the left.

After a while, you come to another section of road at Posforth Bridge; turn left here and pick up the path by the river once more, following the sign for Barden Bridge. Follow this path through the Bolton Abbey conservation area. At the top of this section there's a bench with a shelter, providing a nice view.

Continue along the path, which at this stage takes you high above the river, and you can see a waterfall and a gorge; this is the Strid. There are steep drops down to the left at this point, so take care along here. Go over a small stream and then you have Barden Bridge coming into view ahead. When you come to it (SE 052, 574), cross over this bridge and take the path down to the left, carrying on along the other side of the river and this time heading downstream.

The incredible ruins at Bolton Abbey

It's one natural drama after another along this fascinating walk

There's a wooden bridge you need to go over after 1km or so, but essentially you are sticking to the path running by the side of the river at this point. Keep to the left and follow the path as it sticks close to the water, passing the Strid and continuing on ahead.

You will be brought out at a nice café and toilet stop and when you have refuelled here you should turn left over the bridge and then right at the side of the river, following the sign for Bolton Priory and walking along The Dales Way. Go across the ford again and take the path on the right. The path divides soon after, but both end up in the same place, so take your pick. You'll end up coming to the bridge you crossed at the start of the walk, so make your way over and head up the path to the gap in the wall. Turn left onto the road and you'll see the car park on the right.

Rev. Kate Bottley's Thought for the Walk

Sinners and Saints

Bolton Abbey was founded in 1154 by the Augustinian order, a monastic order named after Saint Augustine of Hippo. Saint Augustine's feast day in western Christianity is August 28th. Augustine is patron saint of brewers, printers, theologians and the Philippines.

Augustine was interested in theology from an early age and remembered clearly the first time he became aware of the concept of 'sin'. Hanging out with a bunch of other boys, he watched as they scrumped fruit from a tree. They didn't actually want the fruit but just desired to steal simply because it wasn't allowed. As a teenager, Augustine took up with a gang of hedonistic young men who often boasted of their sexual exploits. Around this time, Augustine prayed the words "Lord grant me chastity and continence, but not yet". The prayer worked and Augustine embarked on a 15 year affair with a woman of lower class, to the horror of his mother. The relationship resulted in at least one child. Eventually Augustine decided to marry and so ended his affair to marry a rich heiress. Alas, she was only 10 and so he decided to do the decent thing and wait until she was 12 to seal the deal.

When we describe someone as a 'saint' we mean they are kind, generous, wonderful people who lead pretty blameless lives. But the truth is most of the saints who hold the title are far from perfect people. They do, however, usually do something which seems to balance out their imperfections in order to deserve the title.

Perfection may be unobtainable and constant goodness an unachievable ideal. But we can try to better.

Questions to think about along the way

What other saints do you know?

Why would someone want to join a holy order?

Who would you describe in your life as a 'saint'?

Try and tackle the stepping stones, but be careful after heavy rain

WALK 9
Garsdale

Starting from the train station at Garsdale Head, this smashing circular walk takes in some great limestone features and passes an historic chapel-of-ease.

What you need to know	
Distance	9km/ 5.6 miles
Time taken	3 hours 30mins
Starting point	Park close to Garsdale Station, found just off the A684 at grid reference SD 787, 917
Difficulty	There are challenging sections climbing the hills near the start and making your way across the moor near the end
Refreshments	At Garsdale Head, you'll find The Moorcock Inn, a welcoming place for a post-walk drink. Tel: 01969 667488 www.moorcockinn.com Postcode: LA10 5PU
Map	OS Explorer OL30: Yorkshire Dales North and Central Area

Lunds Church

Built in the early 18th century as a Chapel of Ease, Lunds Church – or Lunds Chapel – is now a listed building and sits unused, a reminder of how important the local church used to be when transport was much less sophisticated. Lunds Church, as you will see on the walk, is in an isolated location. It lies 12 miles from the Parish Church at Askrigg and four miles from the nearest chapel to it. These may not seem like unsurmountable distances by today's standards, but in the early 1700s it was often too far to go in order to worship, especially in the frequently bad weather. And so that's why the church was built; it was known as a 'Chapel of Ease' because it made it easier for those in the local area to get to church on a Sunday morning.

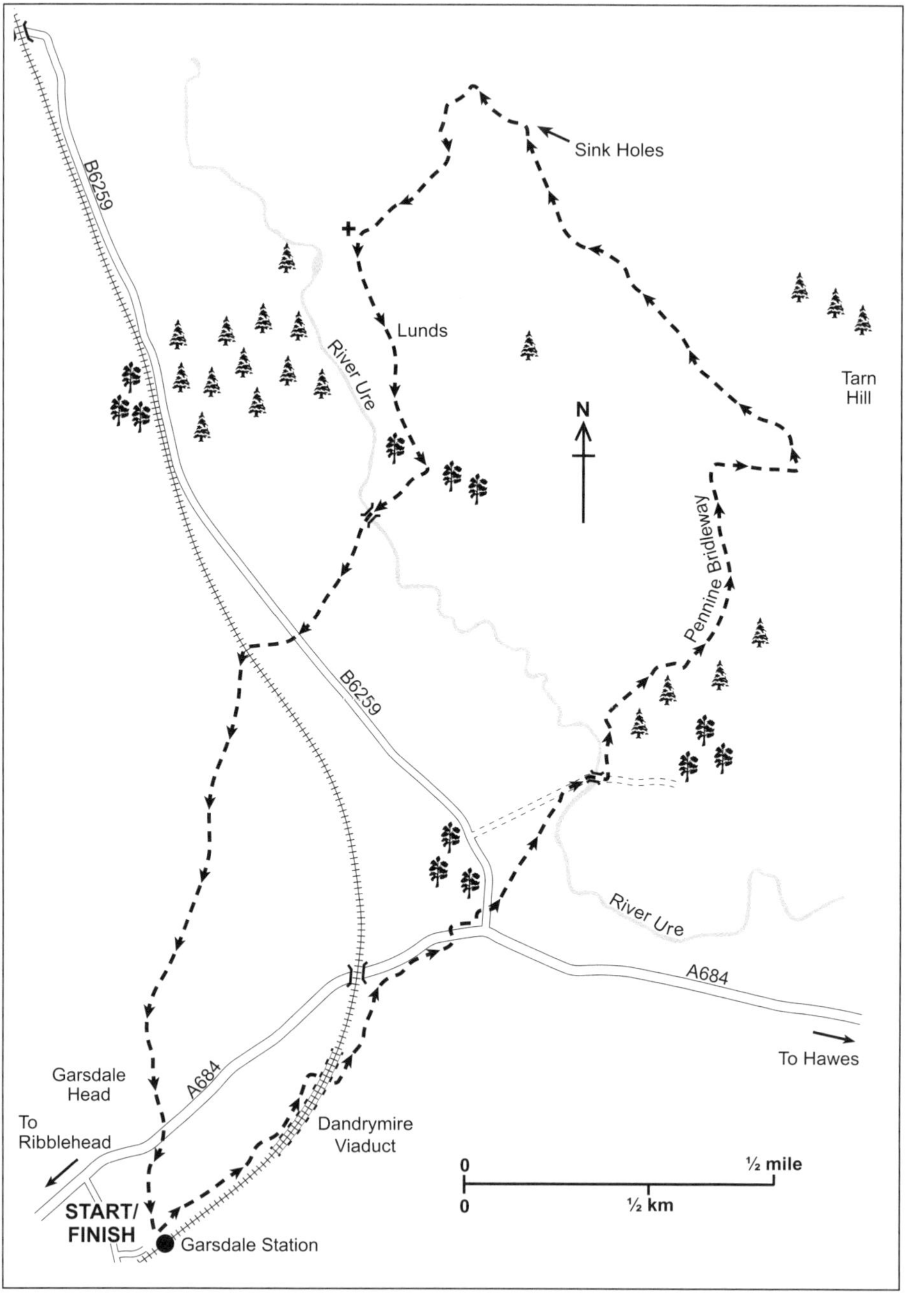
Sink Holes
B6259
Lunds
River Ure
Tarn Hill
N
Pennine Bridleway
B6259
River Ure
A684
To Hawes
Garsdale Head
A684
To Ribblehead
Dandrymire Viaduct
0
½ mile
0
½ km
START/ FINISH
Garsdale Station

Route

The walk starts at Garsdale train station (grid reference SD 788, 918), so you can decide if you wish to start this church walk after a car journey or a train ride. Once you're at the remote station, walk towards the road and then head down the hill away from the platforms. You'll soon see a track on the right and you need to take this, which forms a section of the Pennine Bridleway. Follow this as it takes you over a footbridge and heads down to the unmistakable sight of Dandrymire Viaduct, one of several railway viaducts built to make the line viable amid all the steep valleys.

Continue along the Pennine Bridleway as it takes you to the main road and the pub. Cross the second road at grid reference SD 798, 927 and press ahead as the bridleway takes you up the hill. Follow the sign for The High Way. You need to follow this section of the bridleway for around 500 metres and when you join another track you should turn right onto it. Cross the river before taking the track off to the left and following signs once more for the Pennine Bridleway – on this section you basically just have to follow the bridleway. Cross a ford and you soon have to turn up the hill to the right when the Pennine Bridleway is signed off, just after Cobbles Plantation.

Check out the views as you climb up this section; it's a great place to stop for a rest. There are blue markers guiding you up this section and the bridleway continues to climb, leaving the forest on the right and eventually following a gravel surface. When you reach the wall at Johnston Gill, follow the bridleway as it branches up to the right and keeps on climbing. Follow the blue markers until you reach the gate at the top and then turn left, once against sticking to the Pennine Bridleway.

There are several small waterfalls on the way

The section of the path you now find yourself on is close to a line of shake holes. Continue on here for just over 1km, passing a couple of ruined buildings and several streams. When you get to a dry stone wall passing across the track, look out for a gap in the wall on the left and take the path leading down the hill. This path heads down fairly steeply. Keep to the wall on the right, but before you reach the trees the path bends off to the left. Go over a stream and pass a farm building on the right, from where you can see a waterfall on the left. Go through a gate, head down the steps, cross the footbridge and when you climb up the other side you should follow the path towards Lunds Church.

Keep an eye out for how humans have shaped this landscape down the years

You end up walking close to a stream before passing a house. Go through a gap in the wall and cross another footbridge until you reach the church. The church is a fascinating place, clearly belonging to another time but obviously offering an important opportunity to worship in such a remote area.

The meandering upper course of a local stream

Go past the church and follow the path as it heads up the small hill, then head through a gate and press on down the other side. Continue across this next field and then go over the wall at the other side before heading down into a dip and crossing a stream. The path sticks to a wall on the right of the field, but when the path bends off to the left you need to take the path off to the right (grid reference SD 796, 939).

Follow the path to a footbridge and at the other side, take the route that leads to the left. Follow it up to the road and cross over, taking the path on

Lunds Church, a former chapel of ease

the other side that leads up to the railway line. When you get there, climb the steps to the bridge and cross to the other side. Take the path to the left that climbs the hill and heads over Garsdale Low Moor until bringing you to the A684. Turn right here and stick to the path, carefully crossing over when you come to the first road on the left. This will take you back up to Garsdale Station.

Rev. Kate Bottley's Thought for the Walk

A (wo)man's best friend

Garsdale has its own share of famous sons and daughters, but the story that warms the heart of most in the village is the story of a black collie dog called Ruswarp.

At Garsdale railway station stands a statue of Ruswarp, the collie. Ruswarp belonged to Graham Nuttall, the first Secretary of the Friends of the Settle-Carlisle Line, which was formed to campaign against the proposed closure of the railway. Ruswarp's paw print was put on his own objection as a fare-paying passenger. The line was finally saved in 1989. In January 1990, while out for a long walk, Nuttall and Ruswarp went missing in the Welsh mountains. Eleven weeks later, on 7 April 1990, a lone walker found Nuttall's body, by a mountain stream. Nearby was Ruswarp, so weak that the 14-year-old dog had to be carried off the mountain. He had stayed with his master's body for almost three months during which the winter wind had been particularly cruel. The RSPCA gave old Ruswarp their Animal Medallion and collar for 'vigilance' and their Animal Plaque for 'intelligence and courage'. He survived long enough to go to his poor master's funeral.

As a dog owner myself I'm often surprised by the loyalty my dog has to me but I am never surprised by his intelligence. My dog is not very bright. And although I agree with the RSPCA that dear old Ruswarp was courageous and vigilant, I struggle to agree with them that the dog was intelligent. Intelligent would have been to go for help, intelligent would have been to realise his master was dying and in the style of Lassie the wonder dog, alert someone to the fact.

But doing the 'intelligent' thing isn't always doing the best thing or the right thing. And despite the fact that Ruswarp didn't go for help, despite the fact that he nearly died himself in the process, he did stay and hopefully in his dying moments Graham, Ruswarp's master, gained immeasurable comfort from the dog that wouldn't leave.

Questions to think about along the way

Was Ruswarp a clever dog?

Who would you want to comfort you in your dying moments?

WALK 10
Hardraw

Take a walk to the tallest waterfall in the country before heading to Hawes and spending time in a tea room. This is a gentle walk with plenty of opportunity to get distracted!

What you need to know	
Distance	5.8 km/3.6 miles
Time taken	2 hours
Starting point	Outside the church at Hardraw. Grid reference SD 867, 912
Difficulty	A small section with a steep climb and a little amount of road working
Refreshments	The Green Dragon at Hardraw is your access to the waterfall and your best bet for a drink at the end of your walk. Tel: 01969 667392 Postcode: DL8 3LZ www.greendragonhardraw.com
Map	OS Explorer OL30: Yorkshire Dales North and Central Area

Hardraw

Hardraw Church was rebuilt between 1879 and 1881 by the Earl of Wharncliffe and is dedicated to St Mary and St John. It's a pretty building in a lovely setting, and if you think you've seen it before you may well be right. On TV, the church at Hardraw doubles up as Darrowby Church, which will be familiar to many fans of James Herriot's books – incidentally, James Herriot was the pen name for the vet and writer Alf Wight. This church, then, was the scene for some important occasions in *All Creatures Great and Small*, the very popular BBC series that ran for seven series between 1978 and 1990, with 90 shows being filmed.

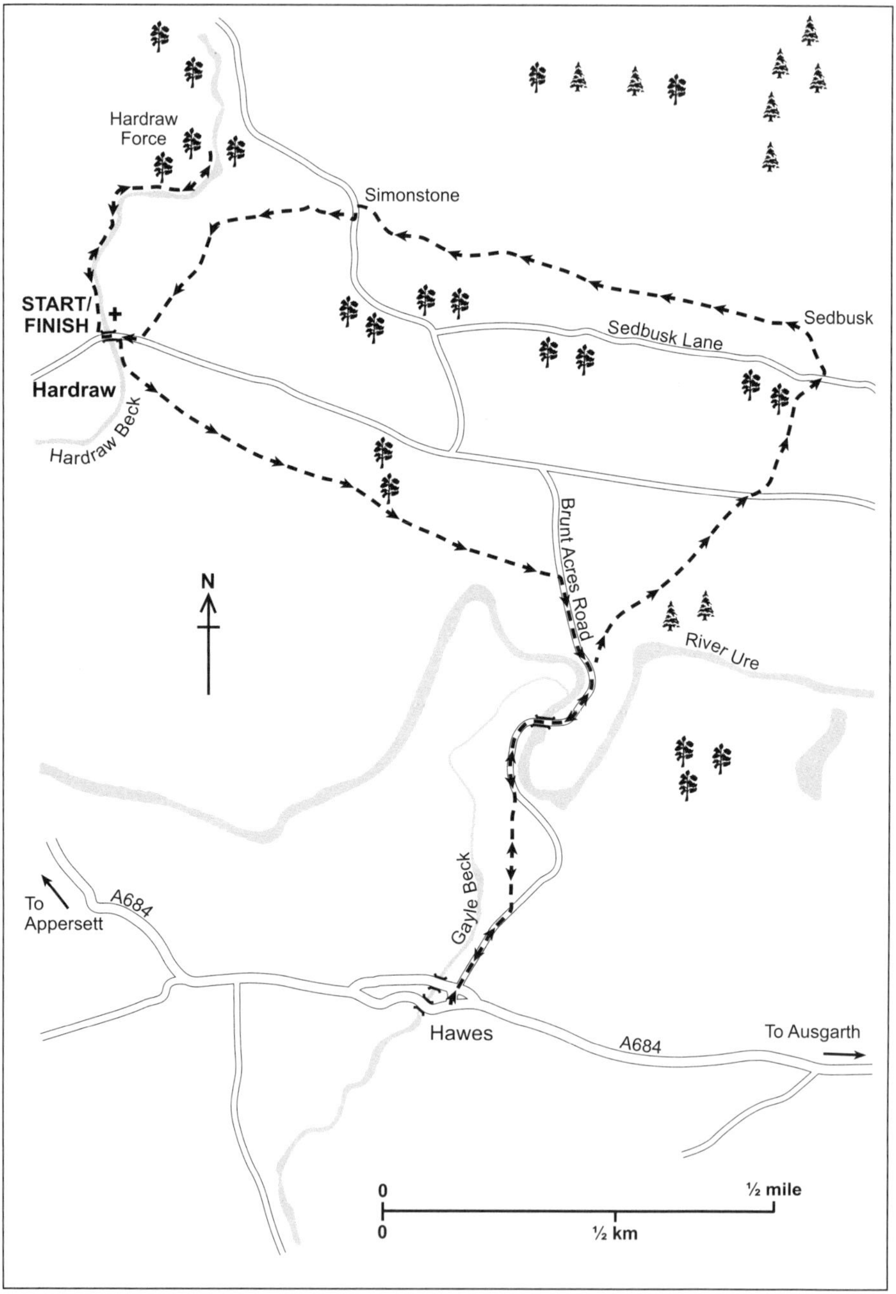
Hardraw Force
Simonstone
Sedbusk
Sedbusk Lane
START/ FINISH
Hardraw
Hardraw Beck
Brunt Acres Road
N
River Ure
Gayle Beck
To Appersett
A684
Hawes
A684
To Ausgarth
0
½ mile
0
½ km

There's a riverside setting for this picturesque church

Other nearby locations to feature in the series include Askrigg, Bolton Castle and West Burton. Many of the stars in that famous show have reflected on how cold it was to film outdoors in North Yorkshire at times, including tales about having to stop filming because the actors couldn't speak!

Route

Hardraw is a small settlement just to the north of Hawes and really punches above its weight as far as tourism is concerned, boasting a huge waterfall, lovely church and nice pub.

Make your way to the church in the centre of the village and, as you look at it from the road, head right on the pavement to the pub. Either now or at the end of the walk, it's going to be worth making the small diversion to look at Hardraw Force. It's the tallest waterfall in the country and once provided the backdrop for Kevin Costner in *Robin Hood Prince of Thieves*. You'll find the entrance to the waterfall by going through the pub; there is a charge, but it is worth the walk up.

Opposite the pub, pick up the track that heads by the telephone box and through a gate on the left into a field. You're now following the route of the famous Pennine Way and you need to stick to this legendary long distance path as it takes you through more gates and fields, until you are brought out at a road.

Turn right here and walk along the road, heading over the bridge on the way to Hawes. Soon after, you'll see a sign on the right for a path to Hawes. Take this paved track across a field and when you reach the road, turn left and then immediately right towards Hawes. You'll soon see the visitor centre on the left and there are range of shops and places to eat in the centre of Hawes - turn right at the main road to reach these. At this point in the walk, take a break to explore Hawes and the visitor centre, which used to be a busy railway for the village.

When you've finished exploring the village, make your way back to the visitor centre (SD 875, 898), where you'll be able to see the old steam train and have a look at the traditional rope maker as well.

The far-reaching views of Wensleydale

Head on the road to Hardraw and follow it for a short time, taking the first turning on the left and then looking out for the footpath immediately on the right. Take this path and follow the paved route across the field. This will bring you out at the road again, where you should turn left and follow it as it bends right and crosses the River Ure. After the road bends left, take the path on the right and stick to it as it takes you across fields and through gates. You'll climb the hill and eventually come out at a country road.

The next path to take is across the road, slightly to the right. Take the path straight in front of you here as it climbs a hill; there are gates to negotiate on the way across the fields and up to the next country road. Again, cross over and take the path slightly to the right that enters the fields opposite. This path heads diagonally across a field and you need to look out for a gate in the middle of the wall on the left. Head through that gate and then you've a series of fields to go through as you leave Sedbusk behind you and press on towards Simonstone.

At the farm, the path becomes a track and brings you to a road. Turn left and immediately look out for the sign marking a path on the right down to Hardraw (SD 872, 914). Follow this, passing the Simonstone Hotel on the right. The path continues down to Hardraw, passing West House and turning down to the left. You'll get brought out on the road in the middle of Hardraw village, so turn right and head beyond the pub to the church.

Rev. Kate Bottley's Thought for the Walk

Every fall is special

Hardraw is famous for its drop. A single drop waterfall 100 feet from a rocky overhang. You can see the waterfall itself by passing through the bar of the Green dragon pub. With echoes of wardrobes into Narnia and Harry Potter venturing through the Leaky Cauldron into Diagon Alley, part of the charm of the waterfall is the journey to it through the pub. Discounting underground waterfalls Hardraw is the UK's highest unbroken waterfall. Hardraw residents are rightly proud of it. But is it really all that special? It's hardly Niagara, now, is it? Sure, it's pretty. Impressive, even. But it isn't going to be used in exotic commercials for hair shampoo anytime soon. Of course, to compare Hardraw's fall to Niagara or Victoria is wholly unfair. Niagara is Niagara and Hardraw is Hardraw. To answer my question, both are special.

The stunning waterfall at Hardraw

We've all been subject to unfair comparisons. Perhaps it was with a high achieving sibling or classmate. Those comparisons are unfair, too. The Bible talks about a person being fearfully and wonderfully made. Although we might say we prize each individual for who they uniquely are, it's hard not to compare one person to another.

Much better, then, to see the inherent beauty and wonder in each waterfall, to appreciate its uniqueness in its own setting. While Hardraw would struggle to have anyone going over it in a barrel or a fleet of tourist boats lurking around its base, it is very beautiful.

Questions to think about along on the way

What makes you unique?
Have you ever been compared to someone else?
How did that comparison make you feel?

WALK 11
Richmond

From the charming town of Richmond, wander through woods, along dales and beside the swirling River Swale in a fabulous circular amble in the Northern Dales.

What you need to know	
Distance	10.5km/6.5 miles
Time taken	4 hours
Starting point	There is a car park close to the Church of St Joesph & St Francis Xavier Church and also roadside parking available. Grid reference NZ 168, 009
Difficulty	A couple of steep sections, but an overall gentle stroll
Refreshments	There is a good choice of pubs and cafes within Richmond, including The Castle Tavern in Market Place. Tel: 01748 826931 Postcode: DL10 4HU www.castletavernrichmond.com
Map	OS Explorer OL30: Yorkshire Dales North and Central Area

Richmond

If you're travelling west along Swaledale and leaving the remote villages of the Yorkshire Dales behind you, Richmond can come as a bit of a culture shock. This is a comparatively big settlement, with some high street chains supported, in part, by the armed forces population based at Catterick Garrison. But by no means be put off visiting Richmond, which is a charming town boasting a castle, a thundering river and a string of independent shops. To top it all off, there's also a small local brewery and a local cinema, adding to the charm and bringing a range of facilities that can only be dreamed of further up the valley.

The quaint nature of the town has attracted a host of TV camera crews down the years, with parts of *The Fast Show* being shot here along with *A Woman of Substance* and *All Creatures Great and Small*; your camera will be kept busy as well during your walk and visit to Richmond, which you must leave time for. All of which means Richmond is an ideal place to base yourself if you want good access to walks but aren't too sure about cutting yourself off from your home comforts.

One of the quieter roads into Richmond

The Church of St Joesph and St Francis Xavier Church

The first Catholic Church in Richmond dates back to 1794 with the arrival of Father Thomas Austin Lawson. This new church was opened in 1868, though the size of it saw the parish get into considerable debt and got Father Strickland, who oversaw the build, get into trouble with his superiors. The Stations of the Cross, which were put up by Father Strickland, were replaced by designs based on ancient Flemish paintings, these are now considered by many to be the best of this style in the country.

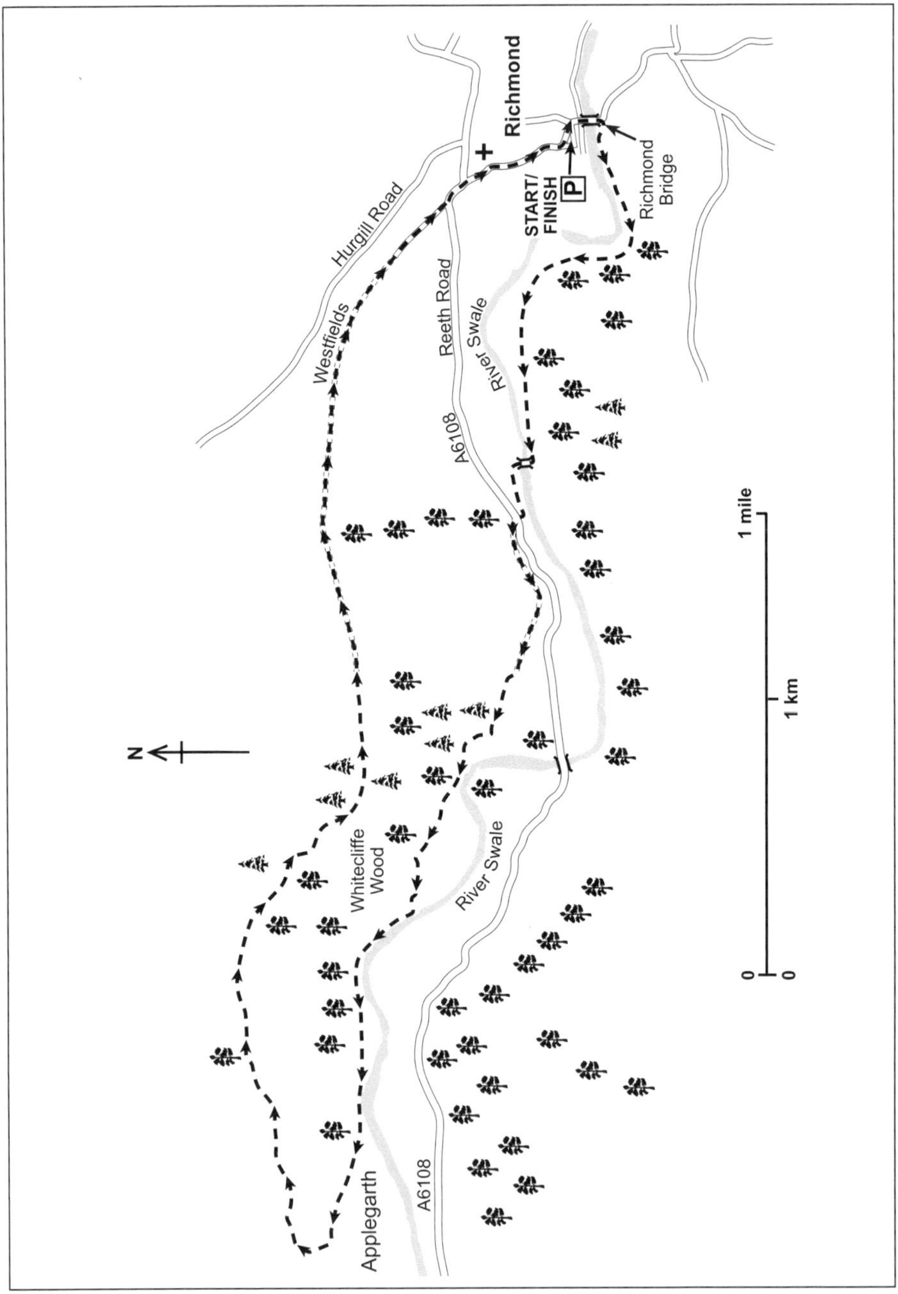

Richmond
START/
FINISH
P
Richmond
Bridge
Hurgill Road
Westfields
Reeth Road
A6108
River Swale
Whitecliffe
Wood
Applegarth
N
0
1 mile
0
1 km

Route

The walk begins at the York Square Car Park, which is pay and display. When you're ready to set off, head for the road and turn right, following the road as it bends around the corner. This takes you across 'The Green' and then you follow the road as it bends right and takes you over the bridge.

Which way now?

Take time here to take in views of the castle on your left and the River Swale flowing beneath you. As soon as you're over the other side of the river, look out for the path on the right and you'll soon find yourself on a popular local nature trail that takes you up a series of steps away from the river. This gives you an elevated position to look down onto the river and you'll soon be heading into the National Trust's Billy Bank Wood; from here you should turn right and go down the steps. Turn left at the bottom when you're almost at the river; the ground is a little rocky here but you'll soon be going through a gate and out into a field. Take the path branching off to the right and follow it into a clearing by the river, which is an ideal spot for a picnic on a nice day. Continue following this riverside path and you'll see a holiday home on the other side of the river, pass through some nice woods and then come to a bridge, where you turn right. At the other side of the River Swale you'll find yourself in a car park and should turn left, walking through it and picking up the path at the other side. Look out for a path up the hill to the right, bringing you out at a road. Cross over and pick up the bridleway.

Continue along this track and you'll eventually come to a farm, with the path diverted around it, sticking to the left of a field before entering another wood. When you come out onto a field, make your way across it, keep an eye out for pheasant and rabbits in this riverside location. There is around 2km of this path to follow and it is well signed. When you pass a house on the right at Low Applegarth, the path climbs the hill to the right soon after and you

Welcome to the Church of St Joesph & St Francis Xavier Church

should again follow the markers that guide you up this steep section and around to the right. Follow the sign pointing you back to Richmond through the gate on the right.

This section of the walk is easy to follow; you go past farms and through woods, but you're essentially staying on the same track and, given that it's part of the famous Coast to Coast walk, it's well signed. The track will turn into a road and you should stick to this as it will soon swing down into Richmond, passing a shop with a Coast to Coast marker on the window.

When you join the main road, turn left onto it, but then take the road immediately on your right. Heading down here will bring you back to the car park - but do stop to take a look at the church featured in this walk, which you will see on the road to your left as you make your way down.

Rev. Kate Bottley's Thought for the Walk

What's in a name?

Search for the name 'Richmond' on Google and you come up with nearly 60 places that share it. There is, of course, Richmond in London. There's Richmond, Virginia, USA, but also one in California. Australia and New Zealand have several. In fact, the place name 'Richmond' is the most duplicated English place name the world over.

A few years ago I read a book by the comedian Dave Gorman called *Are you Dave Gorman?* I can't remember the exact details of the book but it went something like, Dave and his friend had been having an argument in a pub about the popularity of their names. Dave suggested that his name was quite rare while his friend maintained that he bet there were hundreds of Dave Gormans across the world. Dave soon found himself on a quest to find 54 other people called Dave Gorman. His challenge took him around the world.

I've met many Kates and a few Bottleys, but never have I met anyone I shared my name with. (There is a Katie Bottley in the USA but I think that little 'i' makes a lot of difference). My co-author, Peter Naldrett, has also yet to encounter somebody sharing his name. My cousin, Hannah Gregory, once went on a walk through a rural cemetery and found a grave of someone with her name. It left her feeling most peculiar.

Shakespeare said 'What's in a name?' Of course, it's one thing to share a name with a Grandfather or Aunt, inheriting a family name passed down through the generations. But it's another thing entirely to share a name with a stranger. And while we might consider ourselves unique individuals, which indeed we are, to share a name with someone else might give a strange sort of bond with another human being. If we share a name, what else might we share?

Questions to think about along on the way

Why were you named what you were named?
Do you think your name is common or unusual?
What other people have you met with your first name? Or second name?
Are there any famous people who share your name?

We're on our way! Enjoying the route around Richmond

WALK 13
Kettlewell

A journey through Wharfedale, where the Tour de France captured the imagination of the country in 2014.

What you need to know	
Distance	4 miles
Time taken	1 hour 45 minutes
Starting point	The Church of St Mary in Kettlewell (grid reference SD 971, 722), found just off the B6160. You may find parking on the nearby streets, if not at the car park near the entrance to the village
Difficulty	There is one steep climb half way through, and there are also steps to climb over walls
Refreshments	There are several pubs for a nice pint in Kettlewell, including the King's Head near the church. Tel: 01756 761600 www.thekingsheadkettlewell.co.uk Postcode: BD23 5RD
Map	OS Explorer OL20: Yorkshire Dales Northern and Central Area

Kettlewell

For me, the winding river and smashing limestone scenery found in Wharfedale make it one of the Yorkshire Dale's highlights. The journey from Grassington to Hawes is certainly one to relish. When you're only six miles north of Grassington on quiet country roads, you reach Kettlewell – the name comes from Anglo Saxons and means a bubbling stream or well.

It's a wonderful little village and comes without the level of tourist bustle you'll find at Grassington. The voyage on the country roads leaves many

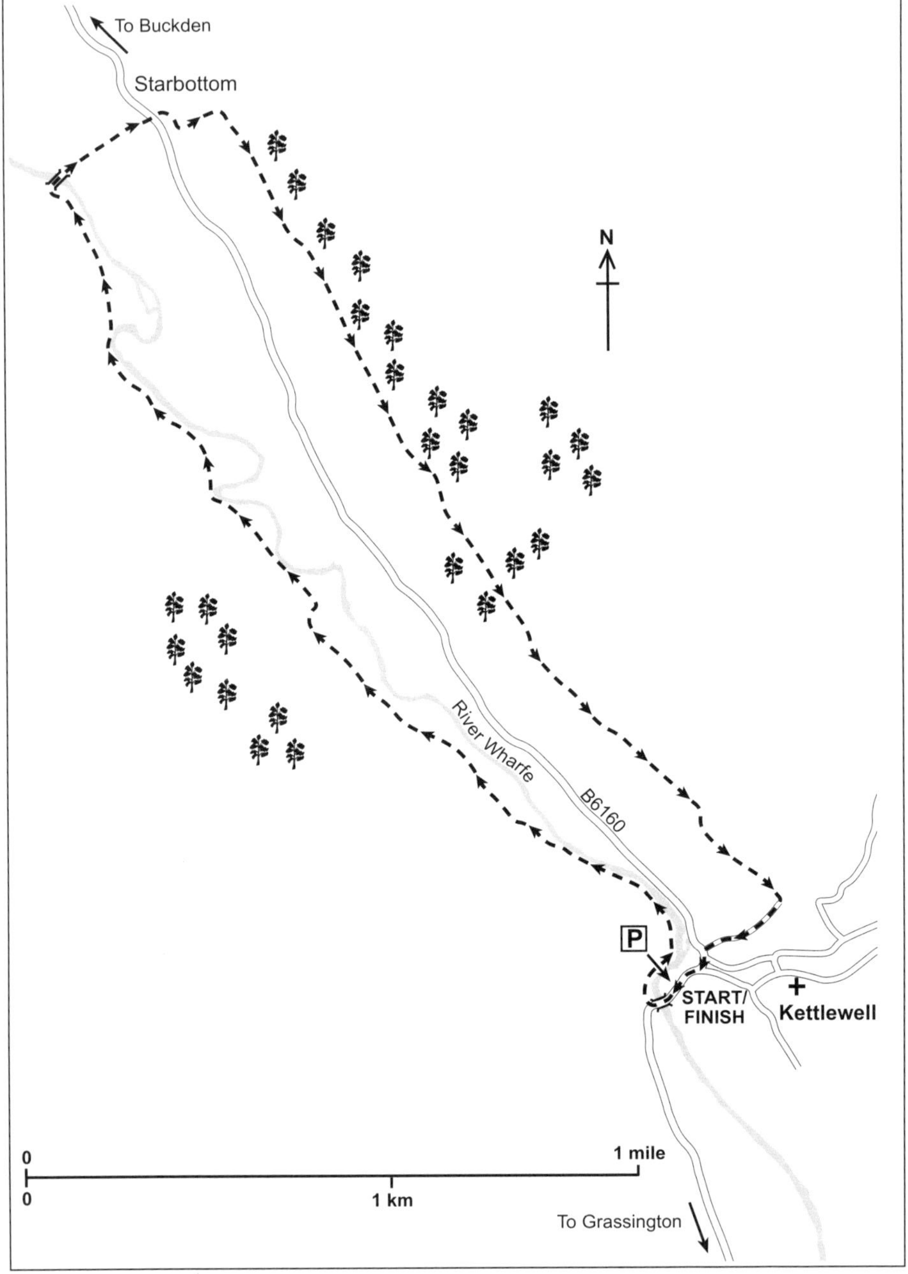
To Buckden
Starbottom
N
River Wharfe
B6160
P
START/
FINISH
Kettlewell
0
1 mile
0
1 km
To Grassington

tourists behind, making this walk - and the one from Hubberholme - extremely pleasant trips out. I visited in early September on a nice, sunny day and saw very few people walking this stretch of the Dales Way.

While you are on the walk, spare a thought for those who were living around here in 1686. Heavy rains caused a disastrous flood that destroyed much of the village and caused residents to flee for their lives.

The church in Kettlewell dates back to 1120; the building was a much simpler affair at that time, although the font with a carving of a wild boar's head remains. The Norman church was demolished in 1820 and replaced by a large building, though this in turn was knocked down and rebuilt in 1883.

Elsewhere around the village, keep your eyes peeled for yellow bikes that remain in place from when the peloton rode through Kettlewell on the first stage of 2014 Tour de France.

The Church of St Mary, Kettlewell

Route

Crossing the bridge and entering Kettlewell from the south, there are a couple of car parks it may be worth you taking advantage of. On quieter days, you may find street parking an option in the village, but otherwise you will have a job on.

Wherever you park in the village, it's a short walk to the Church of St Mary, where this walk sets out from (grid reference SD 971, 722). From this place of worship, walk along the road, head across the bridge and pass the pub on your left. Turn left at the village store and go down the lane that will bring you to the main road. Once there, turn left again and follow the road over another bridge; straight after this you need to take a path on the right. Follow the sign for Buckden and make your way along this section of the Dales Way.

The limestone walls you'll see here on this walk are typical of those found in the Yorkshire Dales

You've now got the fabulously impressive River Wharfe on your right and as you go through a gate into a field, keep an eye out for the limestone scree up to your left. Passing over a stream, you'll soon enter part of the route that is a typical sight in the Yorkshire Dales; a farming track with a limestone dry stone wall on either side. Go through another couple of gates that lead you into fields; watch out for the warning signs about cows if you are walking with a dog. When you come to a wall, climb the steps and go through the gate at the top before continuing on the path again. Go over the small bridge over the stream and follow the Dales Way sign again, which will lead along the path as it goes nearer to the river.

Along this section of the Wharfe there are some great meanders to look at as the river twists and turns its way downstream. When you come to the pathway junction, follow the sign for Starbottom and turn right. Use the bridge to cross the river and then carefully cross over the road. Take the small road opposite and look out for the path on the right (SD 954, 747) signed for Kettlewell; this will take you back to the village.

Follow the sign that instructs you to turn left up the hill and take the steps over the wall at the top. Turn right and continue to walk along the easy-to-follow path as it leads you from field to field, passing through several gates. There are some woods to walk through as well, and when you see Kettlewell come into view on the right it won't be long before the path bends around to the right and takes you gently down into the village once more.

Rev. Kate Bottley's Thought for the Walk

Calendar Girls

Kettlewell was the backdrop for the filming of that wonderful, home grown beauty of a film, *Calendar Girls.* The story of a Yorkshire W.I. which, in order to raise money, decided to pose naked for a charity calendar. The film was a huge success and the story captured the hearts of people the world over. It also spawned a million other charity calendars featuring people with no clothes on. If imitation is the best form of flattery then the Naked W.I.

The small, rural settlements of the Dales add a remote charm to the National Park

calendar was probably the most loved calendar ever. We have had naked firefighter calendars, naked rowers, naked bakers, naked mechanics and someone did tell me naked vicars, although I haven't seen it yet myself.

Being copied can be annoying, it can feel like we are being imitated rather than being flattered. It can lead to embarrassment (think of the same outfits at a wedding) or at the very extreme can be an indication of stalking-like behaviour. But as well as being copied by others I know I have copied many people in my time. Sometimes for something as superficial as haircuts and fashion choices, but sometimes too for more worthy reasons. When I felt shy as a child I would often copy someone I thought of as more confident than I.

Questions to think about along the way

Who have you copied in your time?
Is imitation the best form of flattery?
Is there a difference between copying and imitating?
Can you do any impressions? Who of?

WALK 13
Hubberholme

One of the most famous churches in the Dales, this is in a fabulous setting beside the River Wharfe flows downstream close to your path.

What you need to know	
Distance	5.5km/3.4 miles
Time taken	2 hours
Starting point	Follow the B6160 north of Grassington until you reach Buckden. Follow the signs left towards Hubberholme and look out for the church on the right. Grid reference SD 926, 782
Difficulty	Some steep path and uneven ground
Refreshments	The George Inn at Hubberholme can be seen across the river from the church. Check opening times before planning a visit. www.thegeorge-inn.co.uk Tel: 01756 760223 Postcode: BD23 5JE
Map	OS Explorer OL20: Yorkshire Dales Northern and Central Area

Hubberholme

There are many curious traditions up and down the country, and you can find one taking place here on the first Monday of each year. On that day, fresh from New Year celebrations, people pour into the George Inn and hold an auction to decide who has the right to use 16 acres of pasture land linked to the church. The money from the winning bid traditionally goes to help the poorest people on the parish, and much fun is had by those taking part. The auction is overseen by the vicar in the pub's dining room, which adopts the name House of Lords, and the interested farmers in the bar - or House of

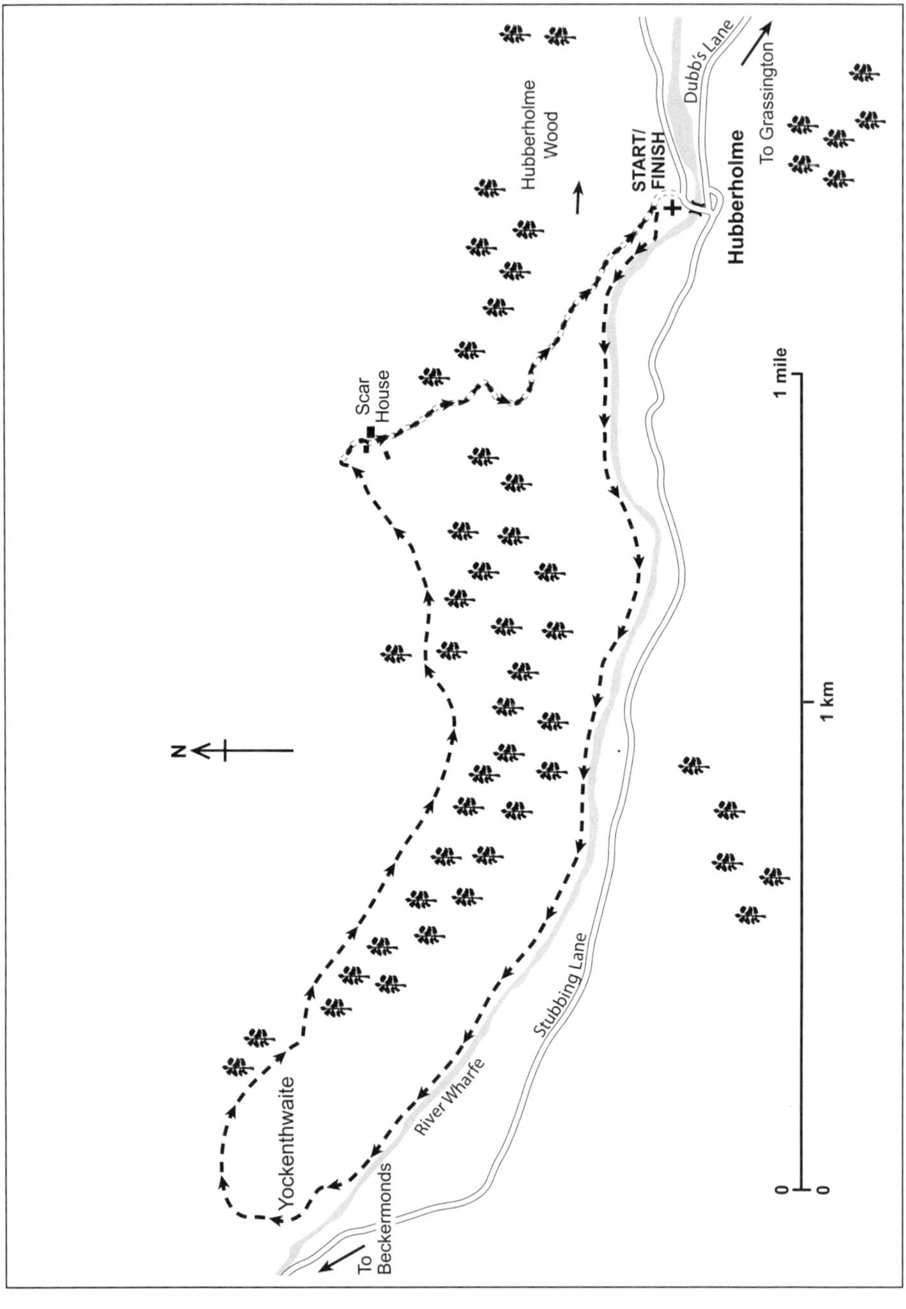

Hubberholme Wood
START/ FINISH
Dubb's Lane
To Grassington
Hubberholme
Scar House
N
1 mile
1 km
0
0
Yockenthwaite
River Wharfe
Stubbing Lane
To Beckermonds

Lords – get their highest bids in before the burning candle goes out.

Famous writer J.B. Priestly loved spending time at Hubberholme and mentioned it fondly in his *English Journey*, drawing particular attention to the "fine little old church and cosy inn". Indeed, Priestly was so taken by Hubberholme that he arranged for his ashes to be buried here. A plaque inside the church refers to how Priestly thought the hamlet was "one of the smallest and pleasantest places in the world". After spending an afternoon here, it's really difficult to disagree.

J.B. Priestly spoke fondly of the country around Hubberholme

Route

At Hubberholme, you'll find the church across the river and there is some roadside parking there. This Church Walk sets off from here, and it's clear to see from the outset what a remarkable building you are setting out from.

Take the path at the side of the church and then follow it turning left along the Dales Way to Yockenthwaite. This takes you to the side of the River Wharfe and it's a simple route to follow as you walk up this delightful dale. There are a couple of gates to go over and a footbridge taking you over a stream as you make your way further up the valley. Crossing another footbridge, look out for Strans Gill

Like elsewhere in the Dales, rivers are at the heart of the character here

As you come to the end of the walk, you return to the wonderful church at Hubberholme

joining the river from the right; there are some great limestone features on the river bed and waterfalls to look out for when the rain has been heavy. Pass an old building on your right and then head through a gate into a field, keeping to the left of it, close to the river. Go through a gap in the wall and you'll be walking on a section with the wall on your right and the river on your left.

Keep heading along the riverside path, and as you journey further along you'll notice parts of the river where the water slows and sections where it flows very fast indeed. When you reach the farm buildings at Yockenthwaite, take the path heading up the hill to the right (SD 905, 791) and follow the signs to Hubberholme. Continue along this limestone track as it climbs up the hill and bends to the right. Take the path leading off to the right, entering the woods, and you'll find the initial section here is flat but it soon starts to climb again. Head up towards a wall and turn right once you're through it.

You'll pass some great limestone outcrops on the left, along with an old building, and also begin to enjoy some cracking views down the valley to the right. There are a few unusual Yorkshire walls to go through here, with the stone built thickly and meaning there has to be two gates to get through one wall. You enter some more woods and then meadow land, before reaching the brilliantly positioned Scar House. You need to turn right at the house and follow the path as it winds down the hillside to the valley bottom.

Before long you'll be able to see the top of the church tower and this path will guide you towards it. When you reach the church, turn right along the path to reach the road where you set out from.

Rev. Kate Bottley's Thought for the Walk

There is a light and it never goes out

This ancient village, which was a favourite of Priestly, has its own lovely tradition. The George Pub has an unusual way of declaring that it is open for business and serving. A lit candle sits on the bar during serving hours extinguished when the bell is rung for last orders. Despite our reliance on electric light, candle light is still part of our culture. Candles are used at times of celebration, think about the candles on a birthday cake or at a romantic dinner. Candles, of course, in church indicate the presence of the Divine. People light candles often to remember loved ones they have said goodbye to.

There's nothing quite like candle light. It is romantic, evocative and has a way of connecting us back to ancient, more primitive times.

In John's Gospel, Jesus calls himself 'The Light of the World'. In Holman Hunt's famous painting of the same name, the face 'light of the world' glows bright by the light of a candle in a lantern.

Candle light, despite being incredibly beautiful, can be fragile and candles need tending and nurturing to keep alight.

For many, faith can be something similar. It can be incredibly beautiful, evocative and with a deep connection to the past. But with a fragility and vulnerability.

Questions to think about along the way

What times in your life have you used candles?

Have you ever lit a candle in a church?

If your faith was a sort of light what light would it be?

WALK 14
Conistone

Once you're up on the hills after a short climb, there are tremendous views and some lovely countryside to wander through.

What you need to know	
Distance	8.5km/5.3 miles
Time taken	3 hours
Starting point	Follow the B6160 north of Grassington; just before you reach Kilnsey, take the turning on the right to Conistone. Go over the bridge and park at the side of the road. Grid reference SD 980, 675
Difficulty	There is an initial climb on this route to get up the Dales hillside
Refreshments	The Tennant Arms at Kilnsey is the nearest pub to the finishing point. www.tennantsarms.co.uk Tel: 01756 752301 Postcode: BD23 5PS
Map	OS Explorer OL2: Yorkshire Dales Southern and Western Area

Conistone

With a little over 100 residents, Conistone is a quiet, peaceful village in an incredibly beautiful setting. This is picture-postcard territory, with the River Wharfe running close by the houses and the dale cut up with a patchwork network of limestone walls. A brief glance onto the hills might make you think there are hundreds of sheep up there, but closer inspection shows them to be little flecks of limestone. It's a stunning environment and is ideal for walking.

St Mary's Church, which you pass early on in the walk, is a Grade II listed building and dates back to at least the 12th century. Victorians added the

Quaint and picturesque, St Mary's at Conistone

chancel and rebuilt the nave and aisle, but kept it true to its Norman roots. The work was overseen by well-known Lancaster architects Sharpe and Paley, who were responsible for updating and building many notable buildings in the period.

The church adds to the charm and peacefulness of Conistone, which seems to infect visitors with a desire to come back no matter what the weather brings. In 1967, though, a series of nearby limestone caverns transformed this idyllic landscape into a scene of terror that grabbed national headlines. To the east of Conistone lies Mossdale Caverns, the site of the country's biggest caving tragedy when a team of six people from Leeds University were caught out by sudden, heavy rainfall and drowned inside the cave network when it quickly filled up with water.

Route

Once you've parked up on the approach to Conistone, walk towards the centre of the settlement. Follow the road around to the left and follow the sign pointing you to the church. You'll pass the church on the left and soon go by the graveyard on the same side.

Take the bridleway on the right, heading up the hill in the direction of Sandy Gate. This is called Scot Gate Lane and is a nice track in typical Yorkshire Dales countryside, with limestone walls on each side. As you start to climb up the hill, you can see Kilnsey Crag over to the left. Continue climbing up towards the transmitter on Wassa Hill, and head along the track as it starts to level out and passes lots of limestone outcrops. Head through a gate and carry on along the track, noting the wonderful areas of limestone up to the left with isolated trees on. You reach a crossroads (grid reference SD 992, 682) and you need to turn right here, following the Grassington sign.

This is the Dales Way and you'll go through a couple of gates straight away as you follow a nice, wide path across a grassy field. You carry on along the Dales Way, climbing steps to get over a dry stone wall and sticking to the signs for Grassington. Look out for the lime kiln you pass on the right, where farms

Few things are as atmospheric as a limestone pavement

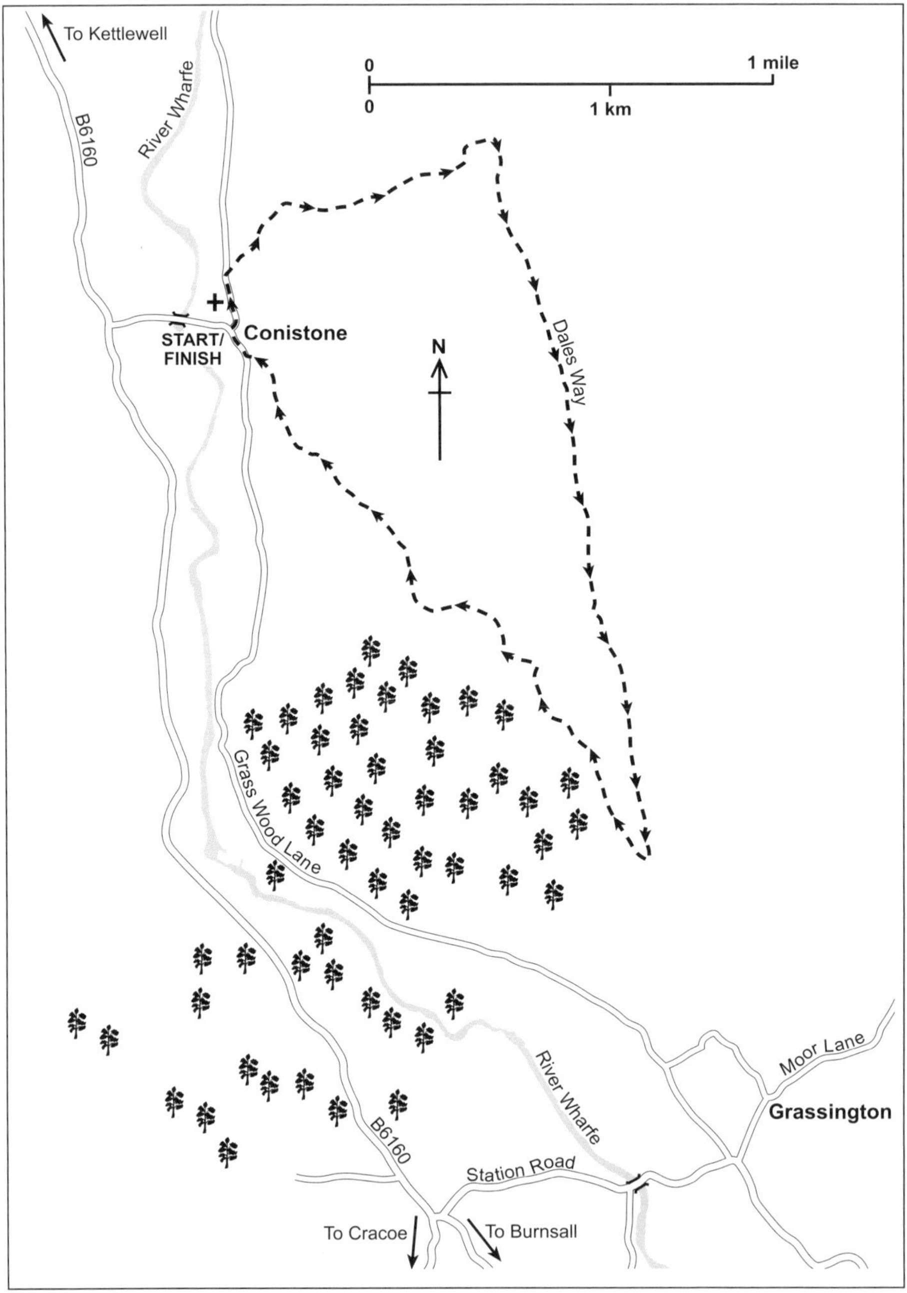
To Kettlewell
River Wharfe
B6160
0
1 mile
0
1 km
START/
FINISH
Conistone
N
Dales Way
Grass Wood Lane
Moor Lane
Grassington
River Wharfe
B6160
Station Road
To Cracoe
To Burnsall

used to burn lime in preparation for improving grazing conditions. Over another wall and through another gate, the path continues with a barbed wire fence on the left.

Stick to the Dales Way, and you'll see plenty of limestone and indeed have to walk over plenty as you make your way further towards Grassington. It's when the village of Grassington comes into view that you need to look out for an unmarked junction of paths (grid reference SD 998, 652), where you take the route on the right that almost doubles back on yourself. Follow this as it bends to the left, passes a wood on the left and brings you to a dry stone wall (SD 993, 661). Go over the wall and turn right and crossing a couple of fields until the path bends around to the left and then to the right.

You're now on a well-established track that will lead you all the way back into Conistone. Turn right onto the road when you reach it, and then turn left at the centre of Conistone to find the place you started out from.

Limestone pavements can be very dangerous places

Rev. Kate Bottley's Thought for the Walk

Mary, Mary

The small village of Conistone is home to the church dedicated to Saint Mary. Whether this is the Magdalen or Jesus' mum, I'm not sure, but I've always had a fondness for churches dedicated to women saints and particularly to Saint Mary. My own church in Blyth is dedicated to Mary and I was christened as a baby in the church of Saint Mary. The church at Conistone has no tower or spire, its bell sits on top of the west gable in a small nook all of its own.

Sometimes people tell me when they visit my Saint Mary's that they love it because it's a 'proper' church. I'm not sure really what they mean, but there are some things that for many people make a church look like a proper church. Bells, pews, towers, spires - but these things are mostly recent inventions, in relative terms at any rate. The early churches didn't have a building at all, of course. People of faith would gather in each other's homes or at a meeting place in the village square to worship and to listen to teaching. Church buildings are, of course, very beautiful. They come in all shapes and sizes. But the church is not the building, the church is the community of people that gather to meet. So even if the building was not beautiful or even if it fell down tomorrow, it shouldn't mean the end of a worshipping community.

Questions to think about along the way

How important are buildings to you?
What is the most beautiful building you know of?
What does the word 'church' mean?

WALK 15
Chapel-le-Dale

Those taking the North Yorkshire Three Peaks Challenge pass this way. It's a beautiful part of the county, with views of the peaks and the equally admirable Ribblehead Viaduct.

What you need to know	
Distance	7km/4.3 miles
Time taken	2 hours 30 minutes
Starting point	The church at Chapel-le-Dale, just off the B6255, south west of Ribblehead Grid reference SD 738, 771
Difficulty	Some boggy ground after wet weather.
Refreshments	You'll pass the Old Hill Inn towards the end of the route, a traditional place to grab a beer that's a stopping point for many on the Three Peaks challenge. Tel: 01524 241256 Postcode: LA6 3AR www.oldhillinn.co.uk
Map	OS Explorer OL2: Yorkshire Dales Southern and Western Area

The Parish Church of St Leonard

The place of worship at Chapel-le-Dale is on the small side compared to many others. Get out your tape measure and you'll see that it's 48 feet long and just 20 feet wide, and it's this relatively small scale that is part of the appeal. It is, of course, a popular church for people to visit because of the location as well; walkers, climbers and casual visitors will pop by while enjoying time in the glorious national park.

You'll be able to pop in the church and take a look at the small collection of local history books that are on sale. Some of these books are about the

Size isn't everything at Chapel-le-Dale

connection with the Settle-Carlisle Railway, which saw work begin in 1870. Several temporary settlements sprang up to accommodate the workers and their families. Over 200 of them died, either in accidents or because of disease, and they are buried here in this quiet churchyard, close to the where the trains still run today.

Route

At Chapel-le-Dale, park close to the church on the small lane (grid reference SD 738, 772). As you walk beyond the church, you'll see a road turning off to the right and this is where you need to walk. Continue following this route along a bridleway that is signed for Ellerbeck. There is limestone to be seen on either side of the track, covered in various types of moss. As you continue, you head into a small wood. The track climbs up slowly and you'll pass a sculpture on the left - the notice tells you it was vandalised in the 1980s and found abandoned down nearby Hurtle Pot before being put back up again for us to enjoy today.

The sculpture lining the route beyond the church

As you continue, you'll come out at an open road and should proceed on here, out onto the fields with limestone outcrops. You'll pass a limestone pavement on the left, which are always fascinating places to gaze out onto. As you climb a little further up the hill, look back to your right and in clear weather you'll get a great view of the famous Ribble Head Viaduct. When you get to Eller Beck, turn right and follow the sign towards Deep Dale. As you carry on walking up on the road you will get to a farm, which you walk beyond by following the path that heads through the farm yard and the gate at the other side.

You'll now carry on along the track until you pass Bruntscar Hall and continue straight ahead. You eventually need to take a turning to the right

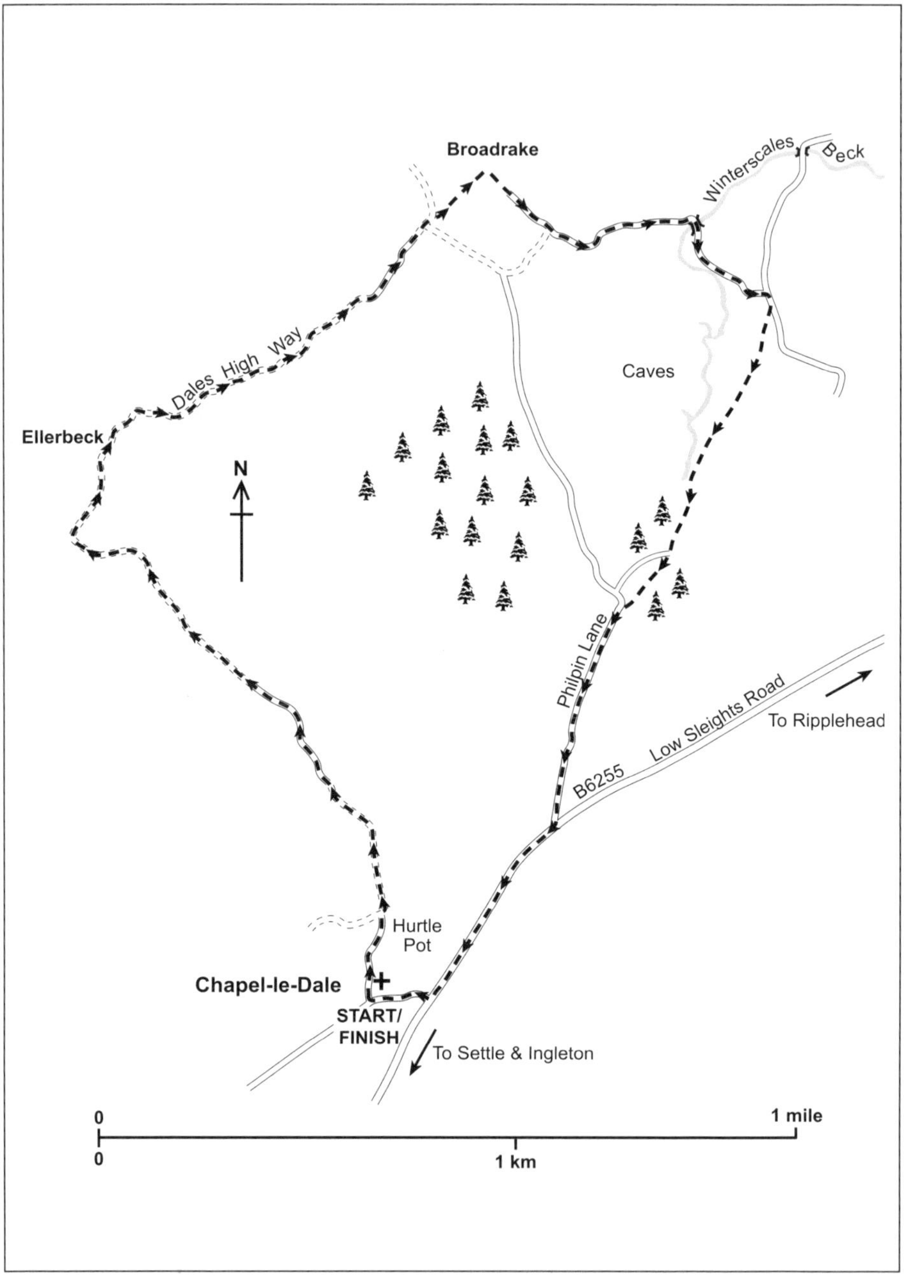
Broadrake
Winterscales Beck
Caves
Dales High Way
Ellerbeck
N
Philpin Lane
Low Sleights Road
B6255
To Ripplehead
Hurtle Pot
Chapel-le-Dale
START/
FINISH
To Settle & Ingleton
0
1 mile
0
1 km

Whichever way you look at it, the Ribblehead Viaduct is an awesome sight

and follow the bridleway towards Winterscales. This part of the route will see you walking towards the viaduct, so keep an eye out for trains crossing over it. At Broadrake, turn right down the track and at the bottom you'll come to a sharp bend to the right; the path you need goes straight on here (SD 742, 790).

Follow the footpath sign to the left and go through a gate, continue ahead as you walk towards the viaduct. The path will bring you out at a road, where you need to turn right and through a gate next to a cattle grid. Take the path on the right immediately after this. Cross the field and go through a gate in the far right corner and then continue ahead as you stick close to the wall on the left. You'll start to head downwards here, passing through a gate; at this point you'll be able to see the larger river down on the left. Head through more gates and cross fields, sticking to the well-marked path. This will eventually bring you out at a track and you need to turn left onto it.

You'll get brought out to the main road, close to the Hill Inn pub if you want to stop for some refreshment. If not, turn right and go down the hill by the side of the road. Turn right when you see the sign for Chapel-le-Dale and you'll be back where you started from.

Rev. Kate Bottley's Thought for the Walk

Faith on the inside

The church in Chapel le Dale is dedicated to Saint Leonard. According to legend, Leonard was a noble man who converted to Christianity sometime around the end of the 5th century. A member of the court of Clovis I in France, Leonard asked the King if he might be in charge of the prisons. Clovis granted Leonard permission to release prisoners who he felt were being unduly held. Naturally Leonard became a favourite amongst the incarcerated and is still the patron saint of prisoners (rightly or wrongly held) to this day. Legend has it that a wrongly held prisoner who invokes Saint Leonard will see their chains break before their very eyes.

I regularly meet prisoners in my work, but usually when I'm stood at the station platform at Retford. You can spot them a mile off, but only because they are all given the same regulation rucksack with their belongings in. I've always found the ones to whom I've chatted to be wonderfully cheerful. They are always, without exception, happy for me to pray for them, often then and there on the train station platform. They always call me padre. I guess part of that could be because when you find yourself removed away from those you love most in the world (rightly or wrongly) it may lead to a greater exploration of faith. Prisons are places with amazing faith stories and many prisons either find faith afresh while serving their time or have a renewal of faith. Crisis, suffering and loss of freedom can give time for reassessment of what really matters in life.

Questions to think about along the way

Have you ever been to prison? Visiting?
What do you think the purpose of prison is? Punishment? Rehabilitation?
What do you think the job of a prison chaplain is like?

WALK 16
Settle

A walk from the sizeable Dales town of Settle, taking in the lovely waterfalls at Stainforth and Catrigg.

What you need to know	
Distance	12km/7.5 miles
Time taken	3 hours
Starting point	You'll find a car park opposite Holy Ascension Church close to the centre of Settle at grid reference SD 819, 639
Difficulty	Some climbs halfway through the walk, but generally easy going paths that are well marked
Refreshments	Halfway along the walk you'll pass through Stainforth, where you'll find The Craven Heifer. Tel: 01729 822435. www.cravenheiferstainforthsettle.co.uk postcode: BD24 9PB. If you're after some snacks when you get back to Settle, head for Ye Olde Naked Man café, where you can also get drinks and cakes to take out
Map	OS Explorer OL2: Yorkshire Dales Southern and Western Area

Settle

The Holy Ascension Church at Settle lies at the heart of the community, just a short walk from the centre of the town. At the other end of Settle, you'll find another building that has brought people together – the train station.

Passengers leaving from here may be heading directly down to the big city of Leeds, or they may be going in another direction entirely. The line north from here passes through magnificent scenery and over a series of

Our walk starts here, just outside the centre of Settle

inspirational Victorian viaducts on its way to Carlisle. The Settle-Carlisle Railway is world famous, and justifiably so.

Today, it is a major tourist pull to the Dales as well as being an important lifeline for commuters and shoppers in local communities. But the future of this railway has not always been secure; in the 1970s a lot of freight travel was diverted to other lines and the passenger service was reduced. British Rail, claiming there would be a huge bill to repair the viaducts, wanted to close the line. This news provoked uproar not only in communities throughout the Dales but elsewhere as people wanted the scenic and atmospheric railway to remain open.

In 1984, closure notices were posted at the stations along the line and campaigners started to highlight the benefits of the line and encourage more people to experience it. The result was a huge increase in traffic during the late 1980s; even though British Rail wanted to sell it, the government ruled out any plans to close the line. And so trains still rattle up and down the Settle-Carlisle Railway today, and it's a route well worth travelling on.

Route

From the car park, head over to the church and then continue walking along the main road out of Settle. You will now be heading towards the wonderfully named Giggleswick and pass beneath the world famous Settle to Carlisle Railway.

Continue along the road and go on the bridge over the River Ribble, taking the path on the right just after it along the Ribble Way towards Stackhouse. Passing the local football team's pitch on the right, the path will soon turn to the left and you will now be walking with the river on your right. There are a few gates to go through and the path continues over fields, at one point with a steep drop down to the river on the right. Head through another couple of gates and you'll come out at a road - turn right onto it and follow for about 500 metres. When you reach the large, white house, turn right onto the track and follow the sign for Stainforth (grid reference SD 815, 655).

Before you get to the river, turn left onto the track and follow this up the course of the river, passing a weir and then making your way by a factory. Continue to follow this well-established footpath as it heads up the valley, passing through several gates and climbing up a hill so that the river is down to your right. You'll cross over a small stream and then see a campsite ahead of you.

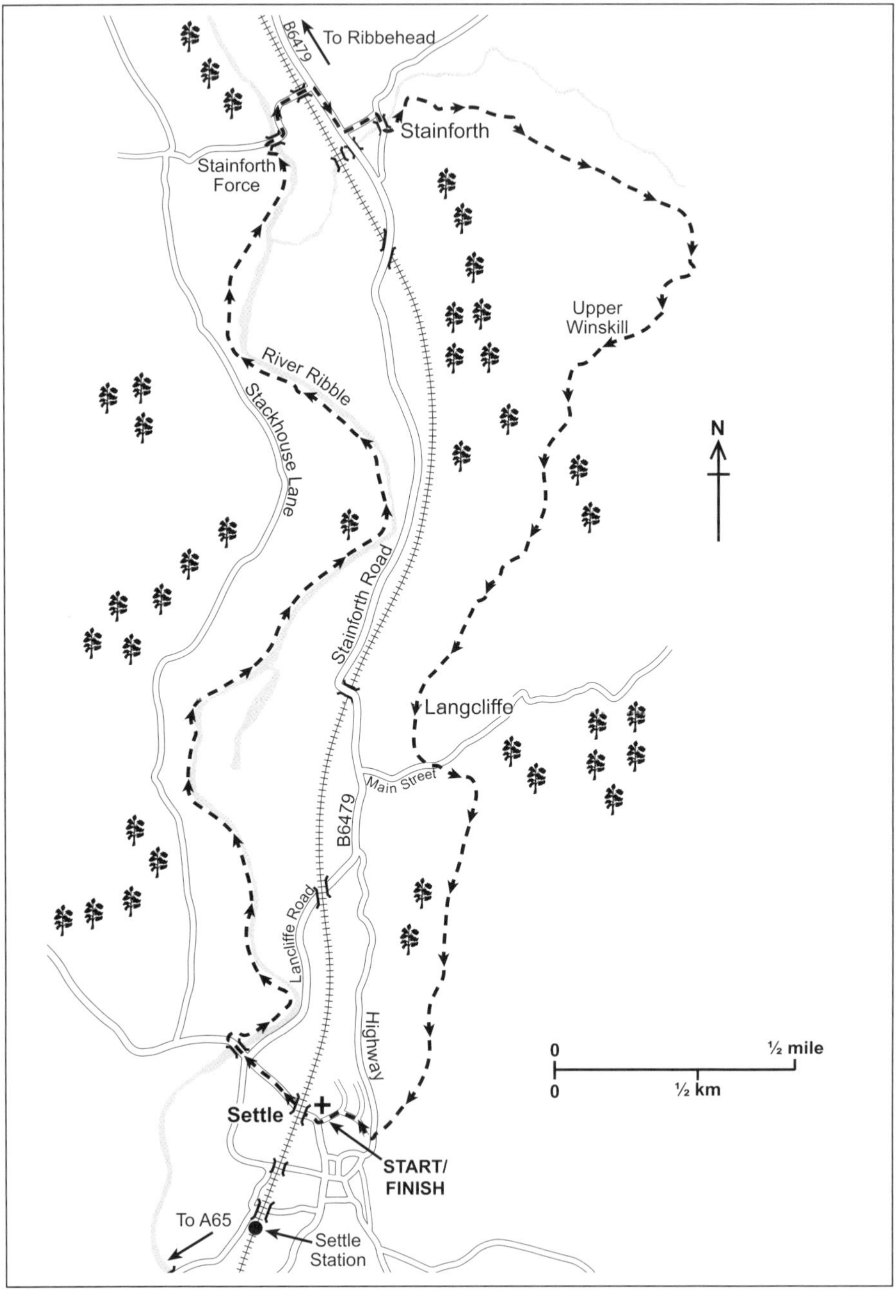
To Ribbehead
B6479
Stainforth
Stainforth Force
Upper Winskill
River Ribble
Stackhouse Lane
Stainforth Road
N
Langcliffe
Main Street
B6479
Lancliffe Road
Highway
0
½ mile
0
½ km
Settle
START/
FINISH
To A65
Settle Station

As you follow the path, you'll come to Stainforth Force, a series of waterfalls that have salmon leaping up them during October. When you get to the nice stone bridge, turn right across it and follow the Pennine Bridleway towards Stainforth. After you have crossed over the railway track, you'll find yourself in the centre of Stainforth.

Follow the sign for Catrigg Force and walk along the road by the car park - notice also you'll be passing another church, St Peter's, on your left. When

This is another one of our walks with two places of worship

you reach the end of the road, turn left onto it and follow it as it bends to the right. When the green area of the village opens up on the right, make your way down to the stepping stones and cross. Once over the other side, head up the hill on the track, following the Pennine Bridleway. This is a steady climb up, fairly steep in places, but it is a wonderful part of the route and has limestone walls on either side. At the top, there is a path down to Catrigg Force waterfall that you can take, but you have to return back up to this point once again (grid reference SD 831, 670).

The Rivers are again a central feature of this walk and Catrigg Force is a hidden gem

Head through the gate and follow the bridleway as it turns on the track to the right towards Winskill. The bridleway turns off to the right and heads to Upper Winskill and when you reach a junction of paths you should go straight on to Lower Winskill. Look out for the path on the left and follow this towards Langcliffe, this being an easy part of the route to stick to and eventually turning into a nice track into the village.

When you're brought out at a local road, pick up the footpath on the other side and follow it across fields as it drops back down into Settle. It eventually picks up the route of the Pennine Bridleway and turns into a more substantial track, arriving in the centre of Settle. When you get to the main road (B6480), turn right onto it and you'll soon arrive back at the church and the car park.

Rev. Kate Bottley's Thought for the Walk

Which way now?

I'm rubbish at directions, and especially road numbers. I don't know my A47 form my B52 and so when anyone tells me where something is I always ask them to talk in terms of nearest pubs, churches, shoe shops or cafes.

Settle has its own very special café called 'The Naked Man.' It's purported to be the oldest café in the UK. Now I don't know if the tea at the Naked Man is better or worse than any other cup of tea at any other café, I don't even know if there is or ever was a naked man (I've never spotted him and I think it might put me off my custard slice if I did). But I do like the idea that this café has been here for as long as anyone can remember and goes back centuries. Places of hospitality in communities are often some of the oldest gathering places. Travel anywhere in the world and there will be a coffee shop, bar or watering hole where men and women gather to chat, eat and drink and where strangers becomes friends.

Although this walk is lengthy, you're likely to see plenty of families on the well-used paths

Places of worship are places of hospitality too and alongside pubs and hostels have served generations seeking rest and refreshment. Some communities of faith that don't have their own buildings will meet in cafes and pubs to discuss the business of the day as well as theology and philosophy.

Questions to think about along the way

What places of hospitality are there in your home community?
What places of hospitality have you found on your travels?
Where did you feel the most welcome?

WALK 17
Horton-in-Ribblesdale

Out of all the walks in the Yorkshire Dales, this one is in the Premier League. It takes you up to the unmistakable summit of Pen-y-Ghent from the charming village of Horton-in-Ribblesdale.

What you need to know	
Distance	10.5km/6.5 miles
Time taken	4 hours
Starting point	The car par at Horton-in-Ribblesdale. Grid reference
Difficulty	This is a strenuous walk to the top of Pen-y-Ghent
Refreshments	At the end of the walk, you'll pass the Pen-y-Ghent Café, which doubles up as a tourist information centre. Tel: 01729 860333. Postcode: BD24 0HE
Map	OS Explorer OL2: Yorkshire Dales Southern and Western Area

Horton-in-Ribblesdale

With Pen-y-Ghent looming in the distance, the church at Horton-in-Ribblesdale has the perfect picture postcard background. A Grade I Listed Building, it is dedicated to St. Owswald and dates back to Norman times – take a look at the complete Norman nave, south door and font. It's the best example of a Norman church in the Dales, though the dominant square tower was built later.

The place the church served was originally known simply as 'Horton,' with the 'in Ribblesdale' being added later as a way of distinguishing it from Horton in Lancashire. The name comes from the Old English words for dirt and farm, so presumably this was once the site of a farm on muddy soil. And you'd be right in saying that there are still plenty of muddy farms in this area!

On this walk, the church at Horton-in-Ribblesdale greets you at the end as you're due a well-earned rest

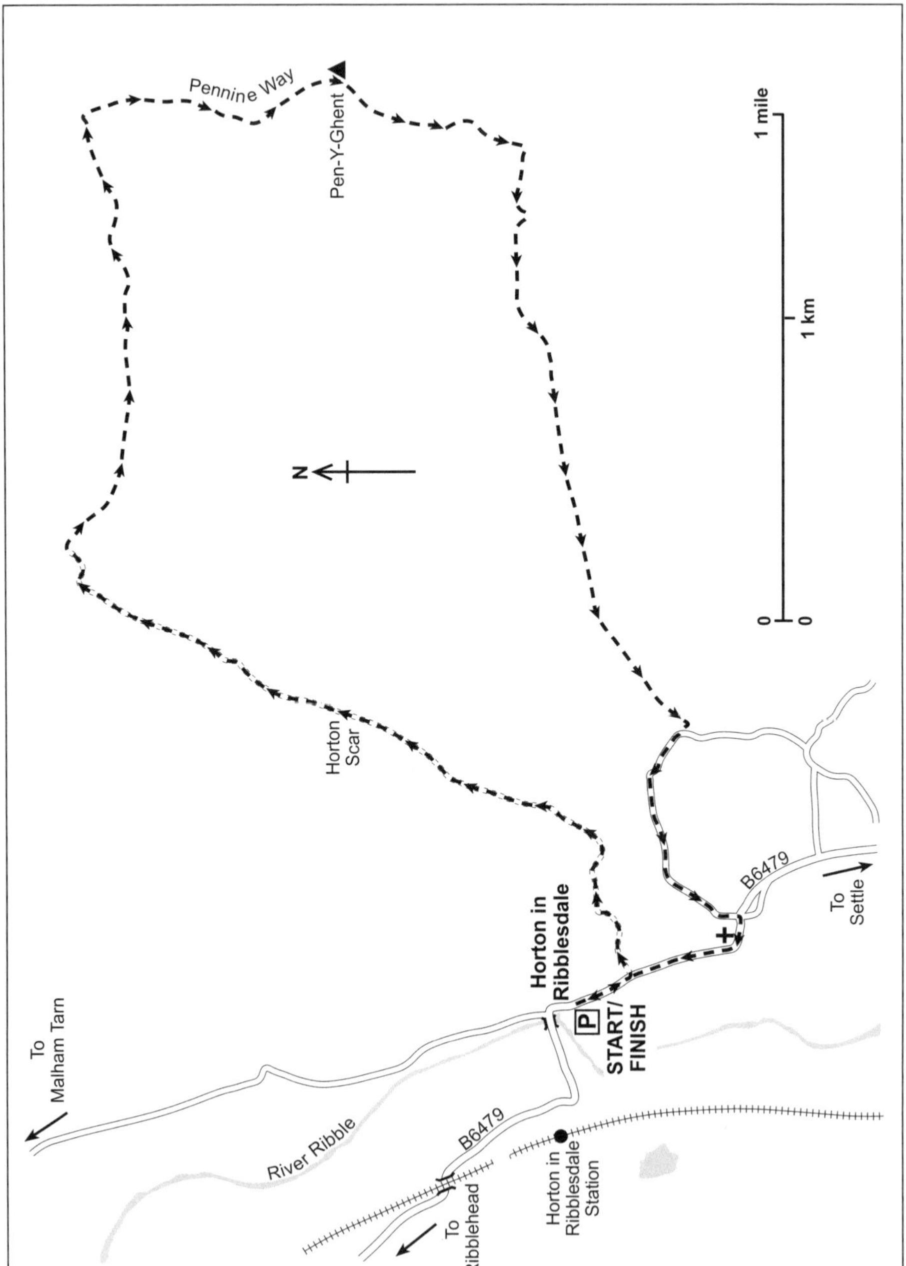

Pennine Way
Pen-Y-Ghent
1 mile
1 km
0
0
N
Horton Scar
Horton in Ribblesdale
P
START/ FINISH
B6479
To Settle
To Malham Tarn
River Ribble
B6479
Horton in Ribblesdale Station
To Ribblehead

One of the darkest times in the village's history is recorded in the parish burial register, which highlights 1597 as being the year when a killer plague struck. There are 74 deaths listed for that 12 months at the end of the 16th century, compared with just 17 in other years at that time. One in eight people living in the village died during that terrible pandemic.

Route

This is a cracking walk, taking in the mighty Pen-y-Ghent and leaving you fulfilled with the best the Yorkshire Dales has to offer. You might be able to roadside park at quieter times, but the likelihood is that you'll be making your way to the pay and display car park. From there, head to the road and turn right. Keep an eye out for the path that heads off to the left, signed for Pen-y-Ghent along the Pennine Way.

Head along the track and through the gate and then when you reach the junction of paths turn left. There is now a nice, steady climb with lovely

The awesome, unmistakeable sight of Pen-y-Ghent, one of the top hikes in the Yorkshire Dales

The long and winding road: Mother and daughter both enjoying their stroll up Pen-y-Ghent

limestone walls on either side. As the path levels out a little you have a great view of Pen-y-Ghent up to the right and the commanding Ingleborough away to the left, where you'll also be able to spot a quarry.

The hill you're about to go up is a serious climb and there will obviously be steep sections, and this begins in earnest soon, passing limestone rocks all the way. Continue along the track, passing through a gate, and when you reach the end of the track you go through another gate and turn right, again following the Pennine Way signed for Pen-Ghent. Soon you'll go through another gate and then need to follow the track ahead and to the right. Through another gate and you come onto a nice track that you can see will wind its way steadily up the hill.

This section gets steeper and steeper and will eventually bring you to a right turn; here follow the footpath sign to the right and begin the next section of the climb to the top. This path takes you along the edge of the hill with a drop down to the right, but soon you'll notice a path off to the left heading directly to the top and you need to turn off and follow it.

You're now above the level of the limestone and can notice a definite change to gritstone and peat. Make your way up to the top and head over the wall to the trig point, which makes a great place for a picnic if the weather is fine. There are a few seats at the top and with any luck one will be free for you.

From the trig point, follow the path down to the right along the paving slabs. You'll soon begin a very steep descent down a series of rocks. The path at this point is easy to follow, but it is very uneven and you will have to take great care on this section. When you've done the first steep section, there is a flat part of the path to follow before another steep descent. Before you head down on this section, take time to look carefully at the rocks; it is here where you are once again passing below the level of gritstone and down to the lighter limestone.

When you reach the bottom of this climb down, take the path off to the right which is signed for Bracken Bottom. Follow the path and head down some newly laid steps into a little dip; when you head back up, you'll enjoy the views of Ingleborough and Horton-in-Ribblesdale. Head through a gate and down a grass bank, turning right onto the road when you pass through the gate at the bottom.

Follow the sign for Horton-in-Ribblesdale, passing a school on the left. When you reach the main road, take a right turn and make your way past the church. The car park will be on your right as you continue along this main road.

Rev. Kate Bottley's Thought for the Walk

Give yourself a pat on the back

Horton-in-Ribblesdale is crazily busy on Saturdays in the summer months, with hundreds of walkers setting out to take on the challenge. There's an organisation that helps maintain the paths and also issues certificates and medals to those who complete the challenge. Everyone loves a reward at the end of their labours. As a child I had a whole folder with all my certificates and awards in. Ballroom dancing, swimming, cycling proficiency; they all warranted their own special place in the folder of my achievements. A friend of mine recently completed her degree and she confessed in a moment of celebration after graduation that one of the main reasons she did it was so her mum could have the certificate for her wall.

We all like something to mark our achievements. A round of applause. A certificate. A medal. A public acknowledgement that what we did was a good and great thing. A certificate is a paper version of a pat on the back.

Some things we achieve, though, are not seen by anyone. But this doesn't make them any less of an achievement. What is the reward when what we achieve goes unnoticed or unacknowledged?

Questions to think about along the way

What awards and certificates have you received?
Do we give certificates out too easily?
What is your proudest achievement?

WALK 18
Clapham

If you're after a great day out that combines a walk with a popular visitor attraction, look no further than this stroll up to Ingleborough Cave and Gaping Gill.

What you need to know	
Distance	9km/5.6 miles
Time taken	3 hours
Starting point	Roadside car parking in Clapham. Grid reference SD 745, 694
Difficulty	This is a lengthy walk, with some steep and rocky climbs. Take care if you go near Gaping Gill
Refreshments	There is a snack shop available when you pass Ingleborough Cave. When you are back in Clapham, check out The New Inn. www.newinn-clapham.co.uk Tel: 01524 251203 Postcode: LA2 8HH
Map	OS Explorer OL2: Yorkshire Dales Southern and Western Area

Clapham

For a village of its size, Clapham has a decent set of facilities. It is, of course, a popular tourist attraction because of the cave and the local walks, and the resulting amenities mean it is also well worth taking the time to have a look around. Apart from the pub, there's a post office and places to stay overnight, as well as nice vintage shop. There is still a train station that serves the village, and though is to be found a mile out of the centre it provides links to Lancaster and Leeds.

Like nearby villages, Clapham was established in Norman times. Parts of the church date back to this time, though most of it was added in the 19th

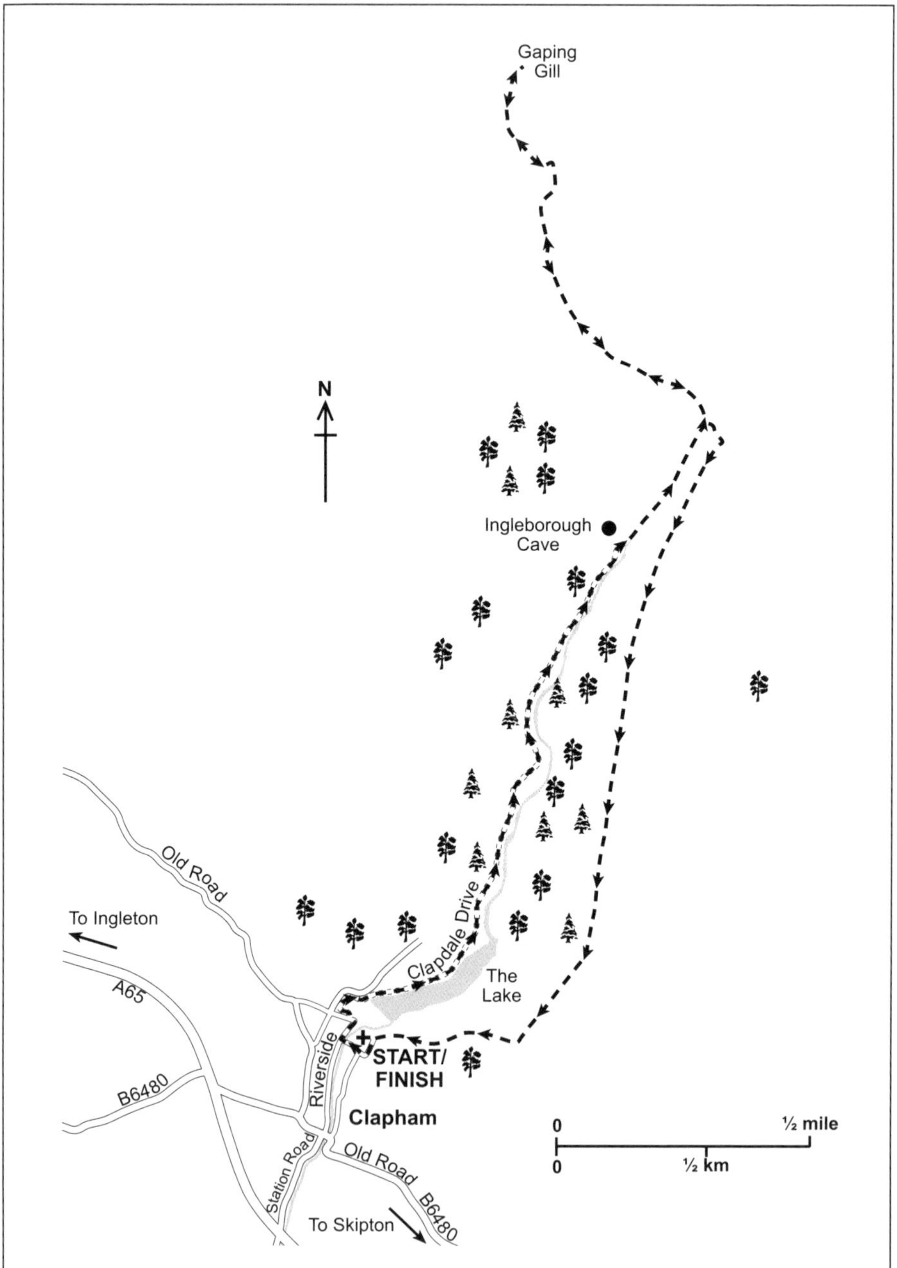
Gaping Gill
N
Ingleborough Cave
Old Road
To Ingleton
A65
Clapdale Drive
The Lake
Riverside
START/ FINISH
B6480
Clapham
0
½ mile
0
½ km
Station Road
Old Road
B6480
To Skipton

century. An earlier church building was amongst many that were burnt down during a Scottish reign in the 14th century, this following the Battle of Bannockburn. Like so many tiny settlements, Clapham has been witness to important historical events.

The start and finish of this walk is the church at Clapham, with the path to Ingleborough Cave setting out from here

Route

Once in Clapham, park close to the church (grid reference SD 745, 694). From the church, go across the bridge taking you over Clapham Beck. Turn right and you'll see the entrance to the trail and cave. And that's where you need to be heading, though note that there is a small toll to pass into the woodland. It is possible to walk a longer way around for free, but I feel the lake and the woodland are worth the toll, which was 65p at the time of writing.

Press ahead on the path, taking time to enjoy the series of waterfalls on your right. Follow the path up the hill as it bends around to the left and enters woodland. There's a reservoir on the right known as The Lake and you can keep it in your sights as the path climbs up. You'll come across an interesting limestone grotto on the left and there's now a big drop down to the bottom of the valley on your right.

When you emerge from the woods, you walk along the path on a nice, pleasant stretch with the river on your right. This is a lovely part of the world, and you'll soon find yourself approaching Ingleborough Cave. You'll have the option of popping into the cave for a look around; book your tickets in the shop and be ready to head deep underground and enjoy some fascinating formations. I would fully recommend paying the cave a visit as it gives you an insight into what it's like beneath these hills where the limestone is worn away by the water underground.

Beyond the cave, cross over the old stone bridge and head through a gate before continuing on the path. Go through a gate and follow the path as it bends to the left. You'll soon enter the dry gorge at Trow Gill. At one point, this extraordinary feature was created by running water in a river that has now taken an alternative course, and it is thought to have been underground, too; the roof that would have covered this huge cavern has long since collapsed.

Climb to the top of the gorge and continue ahead on the path, which will have a limestone wall on your left. Stick to this path and ignore the path that heads over the ladder on your left. There are some limestone rocks that close in towards you high above on the right, and you soon reach a point where the path heads over a fence.

It's this section of the walk that's a 'there and back' to Gaping Gill, a famous pothole housing a huge waterfall that crashes nearly 100 metres into the earth. You'll be able to see Gaping after around 300 metres; it's a fenced off area and you must be extremely careful as you are in this area because the actual drop is not protected. Take care.

When you're finished here, head back to the fence and this time take the path that is on the left and leads over the top of the hill. You head down into a small valley and when you go up the other side you'll be able to see where you're heading to – it's the point at the wall where the path meets a larger track. Head towards this point and then go through the gate and take the track heading back towards Clapham with a dry stone wall on the right. Through the next gate, you'll have a wall on both sides of the track and you'll soon be able to see Ingleborough Cave down to the right.

Don't look down! Gaping Gill is a stunning attraction, but keep back from the edge as it's very dangerous

Hardy souls making the trek up to Gaping Gill

The track that you're walking on is called Long Lane and you should follow it through gates and over walls until you reach a T-junction of paths. Here, turn left and head for Clapham. This will take you back into the village and you'll come out close to the church.

Rev. Kate Bottley's Thought for the Walk

War mystery?

The church at Clapham is dedicated to Saint James. Originally, it was the church of Saint Michael but at some point in its history it changed its name and no one is exactly sure why. It's not the only mystery in these parts, nor the most famous. In 1947 the Trow Ghyll skeleton was found in a nearby cave. Two walkers came across a small hole partially covered by loose stones. They cleared away the stones to find a small cavern below. On further investigation they found the remains of a man, still wearing his shoes and trilby hat but almost entirely decomposed. Close by was a small bottle of cyanide, which appeared to be unopened. The deceased also had a fountain pen, some change and a key. The mystery remains unsolved, but the most likely explanation is that the Trow Ghyll skeleton was a Nazi spy who took his own life. Although no one has ever determined who he really was, no foul play was suspected. The two friends that found the skeleton died a few years ago, never knowing the identity of the man they found when out for a day's walk.

The question of who the man was and his story will probably never be solved. In life, there are always questions that go unanswered. Sometimes we have to accept that not every question we ask will find its answer. But the question should be asked all the same. The Trow Ghyll's man skeleton never did yield his answers and he was buried locally in an unmarked grave.

Questions to think about along the way

Do you like a mystery?

Who do you think the Trow Ghyll man was?

What are the questions you've asked that don't yet have answers?

WALK 19
Malham

There's a steep climb to get to the top of Malham Cove, but the view at the limestone pavement is extraordinary – and the setting for a famous film scene.

What you need to know	
Distance	7km/4.3 miles
Time taken	2 hours 30 minutes
Starting point	You'll find a car park next to the information centre at grid reference SD 899, 627
Difficulty	There is a steep climb at Malham Cove and it is important to take great care on the limestone pavement, especially after wet weather
Refreshments	For food, drink and a place to stay, try The Lister Arms in the centre of Malham. Tel: 01729 830444. www.listerarms.co.uk Postcode: BD23 4DB
Map	OL2: Yorkshire Dales Southern and Western Area

Malham

With Gordale Scar, Malham Cove and Janet's Foss all within walking distance from Malham's car park and local pubs, it's hardly surprising that the village has gained a reputation for being at the heart of the Yorkshire Dales. It's certainly one of my favourite places to visit, principally for the incredible limestone pavement that is to be found atop Malham Cove. If you're completing the walk with any Harry Potter fans, make sure you watch the first Deathly Hallows film again – the limestone pavement is the setting for Harry and Hermione's overnight stay in a tent. And a dramatic location it made.

After heavy rain, a waterfall once poured over Malham Cover. But it's a very rare event

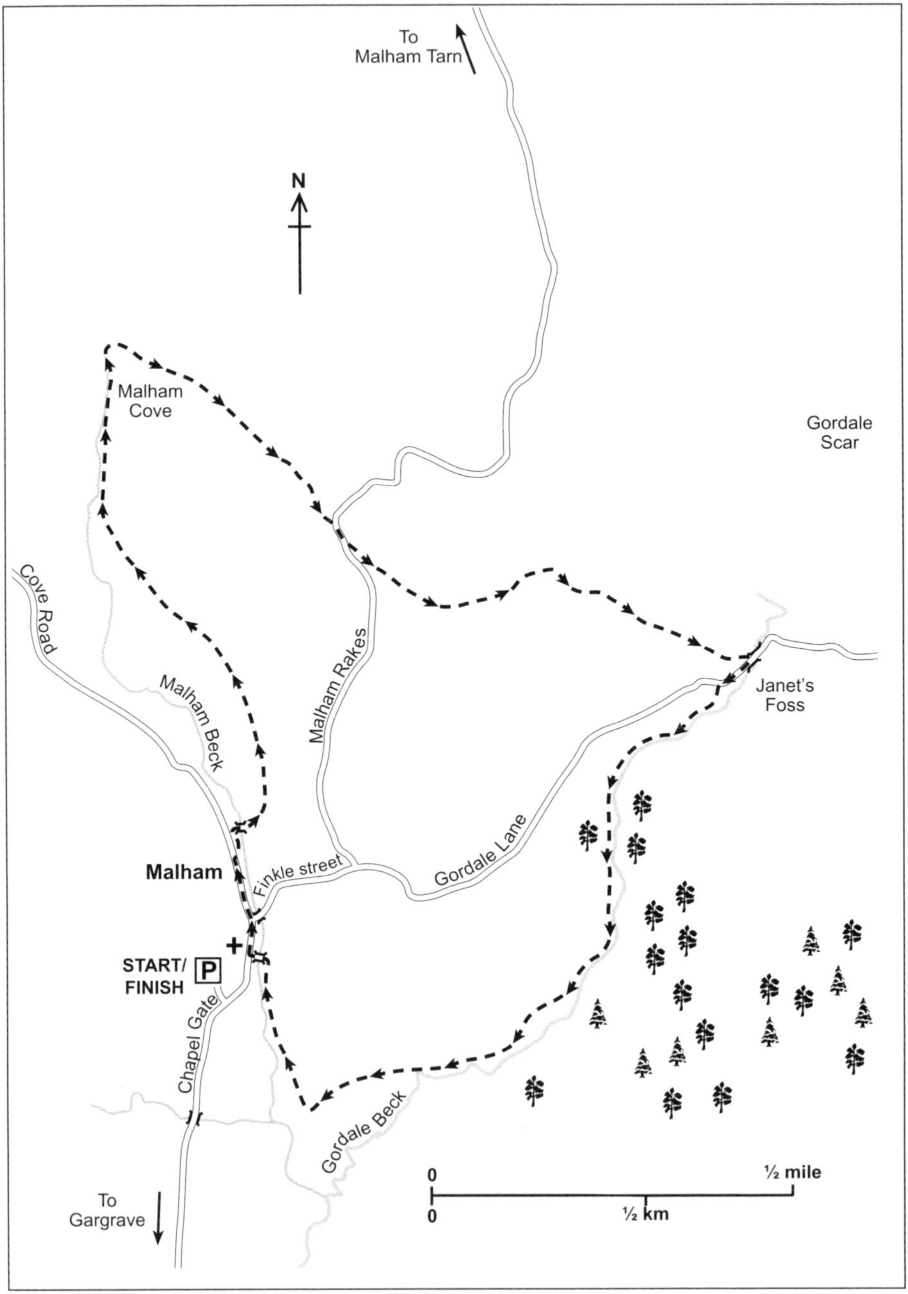
To
Malham Tarn
N
Malham
Cove
Gordale
Scar
Cove Road
Malham Beck
Malham Rakes
Janet's
Foss
Gordale Lane
Malham
Finkle street
START/
FINISH
P
Chapel Gate
Gordale Beck
0
½ mile
0
½ km
To
Gargrave

Malham is certainly a place that can put a spell on you and command your return again and again.

Route

The car park at Malham is easily found next to the information centre (grid reference SD 899, 627). The local church is also found near here, on the main road. From here, walk along the road into the centre of the village. Stick to this main road that goes through Malham; you'll pass a smithy on your right and should continue on the road, following signs for Malham Cove. As you leave the houses of Malham behind you, take the path on the right that heads across fields towards the cove at grid reference SD 898, 633.

Do check out the Smithy when you finish up in Malham

This is a pleasant part of the walk and you'll be walking towards the impressive and imposing face of Malham cove, where there are often people climbing. Before you reach the cove, take the path off up to the left and proceed up the steep and challenging series of steps. When you reach the top, the path bends around to the right and brings you out at one of the most impressive limestone pavements the Yorkshire Dales has to offer. Here, you can explore the intricate shapes and patterns in the series of limestones features, but be warned that limestone can be extremely slippery and there are dangerous gaps in the rock you should be very careful to avoid.

Continue across the limestone, heading towards a wall and a junction of footpaths; head straight on here and follow the path as it makes a small climb. This is Sheriff Hill, which soon gives way to a steady descent down to a country road. Turn right onto the road, but look out for the path on the other side, which is the one you need to take.

The next section is a straight forward one, following the signs and following the path through fields until you come out at another country road. Turn right here and follow the road for around 100 metres before taking the path on the left. This takes you by the side of Gordale Beck and almost immediately there is the roaring Janet's Foss.

This is one of few waterfalls in the country to adopt the Icelandic 'foss' in its name. The path sticks close by the river and you head through a small wood before entering a series of fields. The path is easy to follow and well signed, eventually bringing you to a footbridge and then to a junction of paths, where you turn right (grid reference SD 902, 624).

Harry Potter woz ere! The famous wizard visited here in *The Deathly Hallows Part 1*

You'll now be walking at the side of Malham Beck. When you reach a footbridge, walk across it to be brought out at the village's main street once more.

Rev. Kate Bottley's Thought for the Walk

Listening in to life at Malham

With a population of around 300 people the village of Malham is small but perfectly formed. The comm-unity is a close one and at the end of each August it comes together for the Malham village show. The village show has everything from Lego models to fell running, the usual vegetable competitions to flower arranging. But this tight-knit, friendly community is not without its own strange story. In May 2006, it was reported that a covert listening device was discovered hidden in the local parish hall, leaving the villagers baffled. The electronic transmitter was found in a wall socket during a safety inspection at Malham village hall. No one knew where it had come from or why and, even more mysterious, who on earth would want to listen in to the activities going on in the village hall? To date the mystery remains and no one has come forward to claim the bug that was planted in the village hall.

The saying goes that listening is twice as important and talking, which is why God gave us two ears and one mouth. Some people are better than others at listening, while other people listen well but rarely hear.

Questions to think about along the way

How good are you at listening?

Is there a difference between listening and hearing?

When did you last feel listened to?

Complete with Icelandic name, it's Janet's Foss

WALK 20
Ingleton

You'll struggle to find a waterfalls walk this good anywhere in the country, especially after some rain!

What you need to know	
Distance	5 miles
Time taken	3 hours
Starting point	Access to the Waterfalls Walk and the car park is well signed in Ingleton, grid reference SD 693, 733. There is an entrance charge
Difficulty	This is a well maintained route, though some paths are uneven and there are steep sections
Refreshments	There is a small shop selling refreshments halfway round, and on sunny days you may also find an ice cream van on the route, too!
Map	OS Explorer OL2: Yorkshire Dales Southern and Western Area

Ingleton

One of the more unusual features of the parish church at Ingleton is that it is famous for having a Bible riddled with spelling mistakes. The 1717 edition published by Clarendon Press has a number of classic errors, making the handful that remain real curiosities. This early 18th century version is known as the Vinegar Bible - this is because the chapter heading for Luke 20 reads The Parable of the Vinegar rather than the Parable of the Vineyard. And this was hundreds of years before predictive text, so that's not an excuse.

A more carefully crafted historic feature in this church dedicated to St. Mary would be the font, another one that dates back to Norman times. From the

Atop the and overlooking the viaduct, the church at Ingleton is near to cafes and shops in the village

church, the centre of Ingleton is within easy reach. The whole village is dominated by the impressive viaduct that was built to bridge the Greta Valley, completed in 1860 after being constructed with local stone from Bentham. There are no trains heading to Ingleton anymore - this is a disused line. But at one point there were two stations here, one at each end of the famous viaduct. The rivalry between them was fierce and sometimes customers transferring to the other company were forced to walk down the valley and up the other hill, even though there was the viaduct linking them together. It's now a Grade II Listed Building and is one of many famous viaducts bridging the Yorkshire Dales skyline.

Route

In principal, I do not agree with charging for walks to access the countryside, but this Waterfalls Walk in Ingleton is perhaps the finest example of falls clustered together in the country. Not to include it in a book aiming to collect

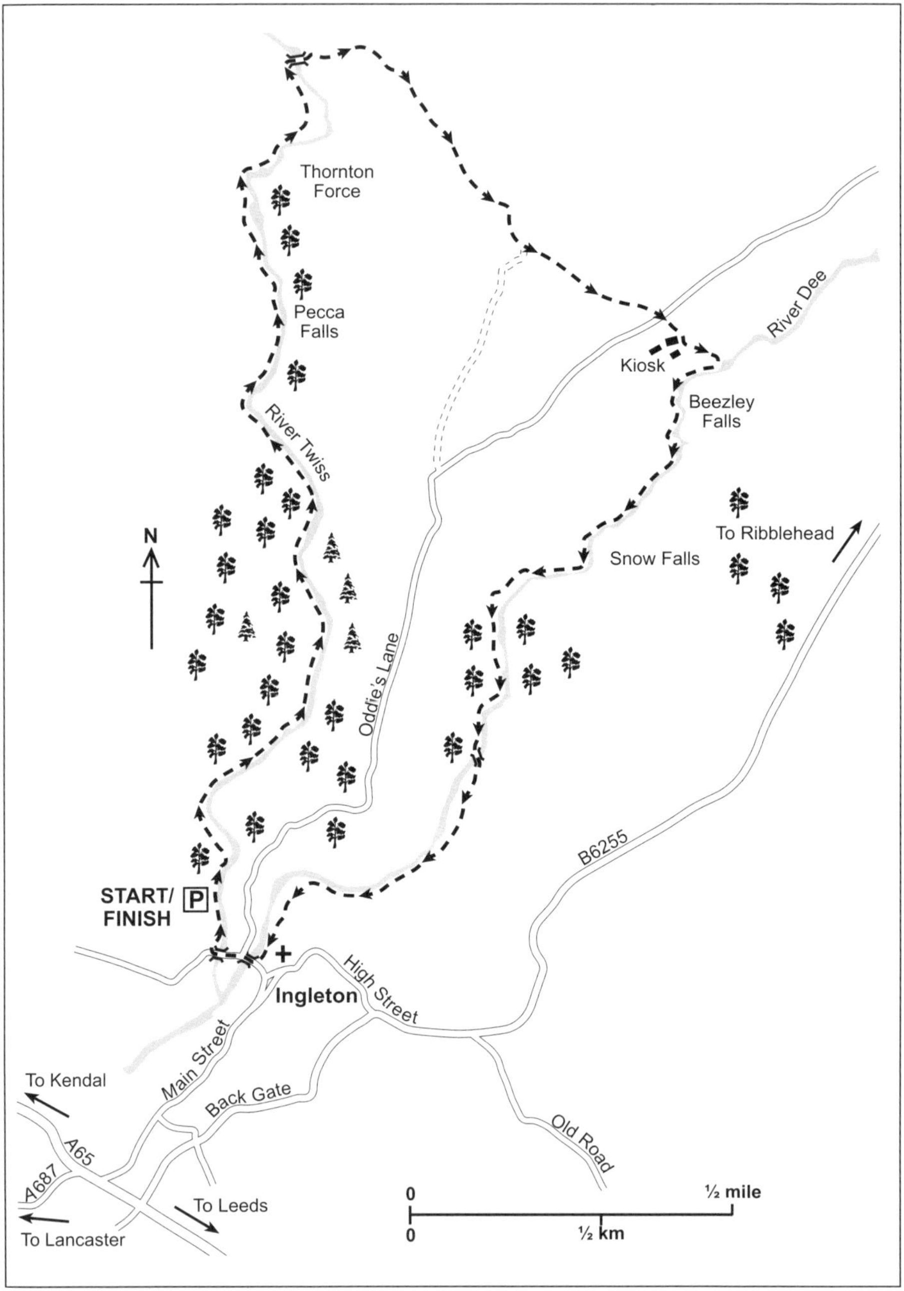
Thornton
Force
Pecca
Falls
River Twiss
Oddie's Lane
River Dee
Kiosk
Beezley
Falls
Snow Falls
To Ribblehead
N
START/
FINISH
P
Ingleton
High Street
B6255
Main Street
Back Gate
Old Road
To Kendal
A65
A687
To Leeds
To Lancaster
0
½ mile
0
½ km

the finest walks in the Dales would be silly, and few people who pay to go on this walk have a grumble about it – as you can see from excellent TripAdvisor reviews. The entrance fees are also used to maintain the safety barriers and viewing platforms, which are an essential requirement. Remember that the key feature here is the waterfalls and so it is more dramatic to go on this walk after a good day of rain!

Head to the end of the car park (SD 693, 733), and you immediately enter a lovely deciduous woodland, with some great trees and the river flowing on your right. Go through a gap in the wall and then tackle a series of steps going up and down, as the path takes you into the woods away from the river. They say money doesn't grow on trees, but look out for the money tree here, resembling a dragon and its scales.

Continue on the track, fenced off from the river, and look out for oak trees. You'll be brought down to the river's edge and you will then have to cross it on a metal bridge. Continue to walk up the valley on this side, looking out for bird life as it's not uncommon to see herons on this stretch.

Eyeing up dinner, a heron stands as still as a statue near a waterfall

Up some steps and you'll soon come to the first waterfall; there is a viewing platform to look out to Pecca Falls. There are five waterfalls in these falls, dropping a total of 30 metres. Crossing the bridge, you can see the falls – look out for the plunge pools below where the waterfall once stood before being eroded back to its current position. Go up the steps at the other side and here you'll get a better idea of how big these falls are.

Making your way further up the valley, you'll come to Thornton Force, which is a good place to stop and have a picnic if the weather's on your side. This is a much-photographed waterfall which, like the others, varies incredibly with the amount of rain

She'll carry on through it all: Thornton Force waterfall

we've had. Climb the steps to get above the waterfall and follow the path – look out for great limestone scenery ahead.

At the top you can see the River Twiss approaching Thornton Force and dropping in a series of small steps. You're now walking in a classic limestone landscape. Cross over Ravenray foot bridge (SD 695, 756) and head up the steps, turning right on the track when you reach it. This walled-in track is the place you may find an ice-cream van!

Follow the signs for the Waterfalls Walk and keep your eye out for the mighty hill Ingleborough as you walk along the track. Follow the signs as they take you beyond a refreshment stop and keep following signs for Beezley Falls.

These will bring you to the second river on the walk, the River Greta, where there are more waterfalls to go past on the return leg. There are a series of ups and downs on this stretch of the river and you'll be directed to cross the river on a footbridge. It's a simple path to follow, with great opportunities to gaze at waterfalls. Sticking to this lengthy route back will

The walk around Ingleton's waterfalls is best enjoyed after a heavy downpour

The iconic view of Inbleborough's table top is visible halfway along this walk

eventually bring you to a road (SD 697, 734). Go straight on here, into the village of Ingleton.

Turn right onto the main road, going by the church on your right. Follow signs for the Waterfalls Walk car park down the steep hill into the valley bottom. Cross over the river and you'll find the car park on your right.

Rev. Kate Bottley's Thought for the Walk

Mistakes can teach us

The parish church of Saint Mary the Virgin in Ingleton has many treasures. The building itself is lovely, but amongst the things it boasts in its interior is a famous Vinegar bible. Vinegar Bibles published in the early part of the 1700s had a mistake in them. In the parable of the vineyard in Luke 10 the printing error reads 'vinegar' instead of vineyard. Bible errors were common in early print runs and despite causing embarrassment to the publisher at the time,

Bibles with printing errors are now considered collectors' items. Some of the rarest command huge prices at auction.

We all make mistakes, but I wonder if there is sometimes a beauty to be found in our errors. It's from mistakes, after all, that we often learn the most valuable and useful lessons of life, even if we only realise that long after. Mistakes are not always the worse thing to happen. They teach us, help us grow and can turn out to be the most precious thing ever to happen to us.

Questions to think about along the way

What mistakes have you made?

What lessons did you learn?

Is there a something to be learnt from the mistakes we make?

Also from Sigma Leisure:

Railway Walks in the Lake District

Peter Naldrett

This new collection of 20 fabulous Lake District walks enables you to explore the railway heritage of the region, both old and new. Follow the routes from train stations to discover both amazing views and a wealth of information about times gone by. You can learn all about disused lines and stations that stand abandoned following the Beeching Axe of the 1960s. Railway Walks in the Lake District is an engaging and inspirational way to explore Cumbria's wonderful landscape.

£8.99

Peak District Walks starting from train stations

Peter Naldrett

Two types of train station walks are covered in this book: there are those from existing train stations that still have passengers bustling about them, and there are those from platforms that fell silent in the infamous closures of the 1960s. Whether you are wanting to reach your starting point via train or delve into the history of transport in the Peak District, this book has something for you. One thing all the train station walks have in common is that they enjoy a fabulous route into some breath-taking countryside. Gorges, woodland, moors, farmland, rivers, glacial valleys and some tremendous hills are all included in this series of 20 walks, linked together by the transport routes that, today and in the past, dissected the Peak District.

£8.99

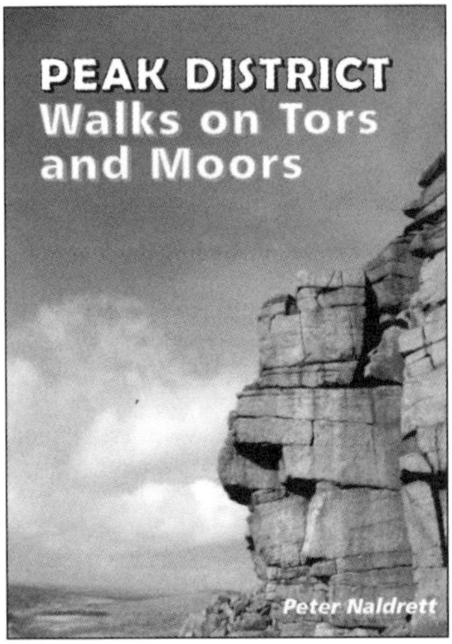

Peak District Walks on Tors and Moors

Peter Naldrett

Throughout the gritstone region of the Dark Peak there are many tors and these outcrops of rock can be seen dotted along the high points of the national park. Although these tors are not as famous or prevalent as those in Dartmoor, the Peak District is a significant area for tors on a world stage. This book features walks to these summits from accessible points – due to the nature of the hills in the area they are a little challenging but by no means strenuous. There are 20 walks to tors including Mam Tor, Higger Tor, Shining Tor, Back Tor and others., together with information about nearby places to visit and explanation on how the tors were formed.

£8.99

The A-Z of curiosities of the Yorkshire Dales

Summer Strevens

Set in some of England's most impressive and unspoilt scenery, the Dales are a fertile breeding ground for the many and varied tales and legends concerning the numerous oddities scattered throughout the landscape. From the mysterious 'throbbing' Hurtle Pot, one of the trio of sinister and murky water filled entrances to the subterranean Chapel-le-Dale cave system, to the legends of the saintly Saxon princess strangled with her own plaits, the hidden treasure guarded by a ferocious phantom chicken and the 'Devil's Mustard Mill' to name but a few, this plentifully illustrated, informative, amusing and definitely quirky compendium is bound to delight residents, visitors and the armchair explorer alike.

£8.99

Rocky Rambles in the Yorkshire Dales

Dyfed Evans

This book is intended for the walker who has an appreciation of the natural landscape and an interest in how it has developed over time. It is divided into two parts: the first part provides simplified information on the geological history of the Yorkshire Dales. It then presents 14 recommended walks, of varying lengths, where the effects of the underlying geology can be easily seen and where the subsequent processes of erosion can be understood in finer detail. The walks are also in areas where the natural beauty of the Dales can be seen to its full extent and its shaping can be better appreciated.

£8.99

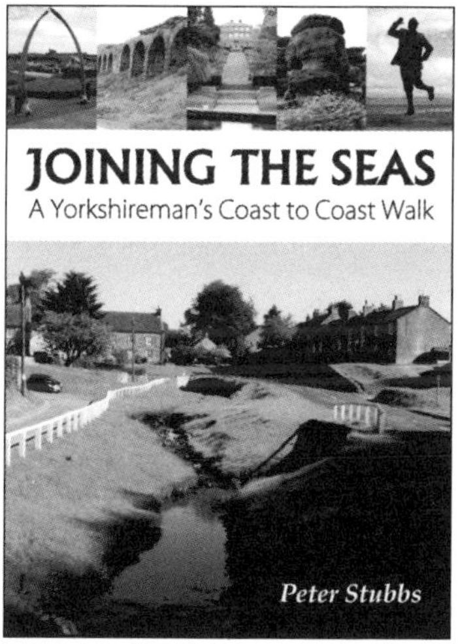

Joining the Seas

A Yorkshireman's Coast to Coast Walk

Peter Stubbs

An alternative to Wainwright's iconic Coast-to-Coast walk, this 150-mile trek across northern England focuses on some of the historic towns and villages, ruined abbeys and stunning landscape features of Yorkshire, voted third in the list of top 10 world regions to visit in Lonely Planet's Best in Travel guide for 2014. Beginning at Whitby the walk traverses the North York Moors, the Vale of York, the Nidderdale Area of Outstanding Natural Beauty, the Yorkshire Dales and the northern edge of the Forest of Bowland, before finishing with a short hop through Lancashire at its narrowest point to reach Morecambe on the West coast. The walk has been divided into seventeen stages, varying in length from less than four to around 15 miles that can be combined to suit individual tastes.

£8.99

Yorkshire Walks
6 Dales — 30 Walks
John Burland

John Burland, the founder of the Wainwright Society and a regular contributor to Cumbria & Dalesman magazines has written a book containing 30 walks in the Yorkshire Dales, located in the six dales of Ribblesdale, Airedale, Wharfedale, Nidderdale, Wensleydale and Swaledale. The book contains walks varying from four miles to twelve miles with various levels of difficulty to suit all types of walker. The routes have been selected to give a wide variety in terms of both distance and ascent. This was done deliberately to add as much variety to the book as possible, and to encourage all types of walkers to use the book.

£8.99

Yorkshire Dales Trigpointing Walks
hill walking with a point to it!

Keith Stevens

This book introduces the pastime of trigpointing, with 25 walks in the Yorkshire Dales, each aimed at finding Ordnance Survey pillars.They're just pyramids of stone, nothing to right home about, but they're part of our heritage and worthy of our patronage. It's an excuse to get out in the fresh air and try out some new ground, with the objective of reaching the pillars adding a new dimension to the walking experience.

The walks are for all ramblers, experienced or otherwise, some easy and others more challenging. Walk to all the best scenic viewpoints — from the top you can spot all the surrounding pillars. This book shows you how.

£9.99

Adventure Walks for Little Explorers in the Yorkshire Dales

Rebecca Chippindale and Rebecca Terry

This isn't just a book of fifteen walks for small children – it's an all-inclusive family adventure. Grab your 'Kit' and prepare to open up your senses. Feel parts of the journey, magnify the Yorkshire Dales, collect items along the way and create something different when you get home.

£8.99

Historical Walks through Lancashire and Yorkshire

Tom Schofield

The counties of Lancashire and Yorkshire abound with places of history and interest, some of which will be glimpsed in the course of these walks. The thirty three linked circular walks begin and end in the ancient county cities of Lancaster and York and include visits to the sites of seven castles and three abbeys. The guide has been designed to cater for both the dedicated long distance walker and also the family rambler. With the inclusion of the return routes, the guide gives the walker the opportunity to complete a long distance route over a period of time, whilst attaining a wider experience of the local area. When passing through a number of towns and larger villages, the routes have been carefully designed to keep road walking to a minimum, but without loss of their particular interest and character.

£8.99